CW00542048

ECCLES & SWINTON
THROUGH TIME
Steven Dickens

AMBERLEY

First published 2015

Amberley Publishing
The Hill, Stroud, Gloucestershire, GL5 4EP
www.amberley-books.com

Copyright © Steven Dickens, 2015

The right of Steven Dickens to be identified as the
Author of this work has been asserted in accordance with
the Copyrights, Designs and Patents Act 1988.

ISBN 978 1 4456 2094 7 (print)
ISBN 978 1 4456 2104 3 (ebook)

All rights reserved. No part of this book may be reprinted
or reproduced or utilised in any form or by any electronic,
mechanical or other means, now known or hereafter
invented, including photocopying and recording, or in
any information storage or retrieval system, without the
permission in writing from the Publishers.

British Library Cataloguing in Publication Data.
A catalogue record for this book is available from the
British Library.

Typesetting by Amberley Publishing.
Printed in Great Britain.

Introduction

Eccles derives its name from the ancient word for church. The parish church of St Mary, dating back to Norman times, has played a central role in the history and development of the town, as well as the surrounding townships of Pendleton, Barton, Monton and Winton, all originally Saxon settlements. Eccles does not appear in the *Domesday Book*, but the neighbouring manor of Barton has still had an influential effect upon Eccles, with the Booth, de Trafford, Worsley and Brereton families figuring in its history. The influence of my own family on the district lies with Edward Hallsworth, a Liberal councillor, and Alderman in Eccles for around forty years (1890s to 1930s).

Agriculture predominated until the latter part of the eighteenth century and the construction of the Bridgewater Canal by the Duke of Bridgewater and his renowned engineer, James Brindley. Brindley's aqueduct over the River Irwell was a major feat of engineering, opening in 1761. Later, in 1894, the Manchester Ship Canal further transformed the area. In 1830, the Liverpool and Manchester Railway was constructed through Eccles. The world's first passenger railway service will also be noted for the opening day accident, which saw William Huskisson, MP, knocked down and seriously injured by a steam engine. He was taken to Eccles vicarage, where he later died.

Soon after these developments in transport, the industrialisation of Eccles began in earnest. Silk mills and then cotton mills were established. The population and housing stock, some of which still survives, rose in order to service these new industries. However, these were not the only industrial activities the district had to offer. In 1836, the Scottish engineer, James Nasmyth, who invented the steam hammer, opened his iron foundry at Patricroft. Here he produced machine tools and steam locomotives, many being exported around the world in order to provide transport infrastructure for the British Empire. In 1873, the Protector Lamp and Lighting Co. Ltd was formed. They developed the first motor-driven fire engine in the country. The town is also noted for its 'Eccles Cakes'.

The Barton, Eccles, Winton and Monton Local Board of Health was formed in 1854. In 1892, a Charter of Incorporation was granted to Eccles, which remained a municipal borough until the end of March 1974, when it became a part of the City of Salford. Neighbouring Swinton, whose name is derived from the practice of pig farming in the area, belonged to Whalley Abbey in the Middle Ages. Its lands were later granted to Thurston Tyldesley of Wardley Hall, with some areas remaining in the possession of the Knights Hospitallers. In more recent times, Swinton District Local Board of Health was set up in 1867, being renamed Swinton and Pendlebury Local Board of Health in 1869. In 1894, Swinton and Pendlebury became urban districts of Lancashire, finally becoming a Municipal Borough in 1934. Then in March 1974, Swinton and Pendlebury became a part of the City of Salford and today benefit from its position as the seat of Salford City Council, with its base at Salford Civic Centre, formerly Swinton Town Hall, on Chorley Road, Swinton.

Until the onset of the Industrial Revolution, *c.* 1750, Swinton was ostensibly an area dominated by the practice of agriculture. Coal mining led to the establishment of Swinton as an important industrial area, with Agecroft Colliery influencing the local economy. The practices of cotton spinning and brick making benefitted from the presence of coal both for power and as a raw material. Inevitably, industrial growth led to urban expansion and the development of roads and railways, which saw much of the rural estate of Swinton Park given over for development, as the nineteenth and early twentieth centuries progressed. As a result of these developments, Swinton has become an important commuter town, due to its well-developed local transport network of roads and railways, including the A580 East Lancashire Road, which opened in 1934. My own relatives, the Cliffe family, lived at Parkgate Drive, with members of the Litt family at Manor Road and Cliftonville Drive, in this period of growth and development.

Swinton has a history of success in the sport of Rugby League, with Swinton RLFC achieving six Championships and three Challenge Cup wins, which is a better record than their local rivals, Salford RLFC. Pendlebury is noted for the Children's Hospital, which occupied a site around Hospital Road from 1873 until its closure on 27 June 2009. The site is now being developed, while the hospital has moved to a 'state-of-the-art' facility at the new Royal Manchester Children's Hospital on Oxford Road.

Over the years, the area covered by this book has changed a great deal, and it has not always been possible to take a modern photograph at exactly the same location as its original counterpart. Where this is the case, the nearest recognisable location to the original has been chosen, with Christ Church at Pendlebury, a notable example. Where trees and buildings obscure the view from Bolton Road, Christ Church has been photographed from Pendlebury Road, as an alternative location. Station Road, Pendlebury, at the former site of Swinton RLFC, has been photographed, although the ground was to be found off the main road at this point, behind Swinton railway station. The club house at Worsley Golf Club is shown at Stableford Avenue, from the end of this private road and showing the rear of the club house in the modern view. Gilda Brook Road is much changed since the advent of the M602 motorway and road widening to accommodate motor traffic and so the modern view is a general panorama of the area. Finally, the extensive area covered by Patricroft Railway Yard is now an industrial estate, so focus has been switched to Patricroft station. Despite these challenges, the final outcome has been a positive one and I hope you, the reader, enjoy this selection of Eccles and Swinton Through Time.

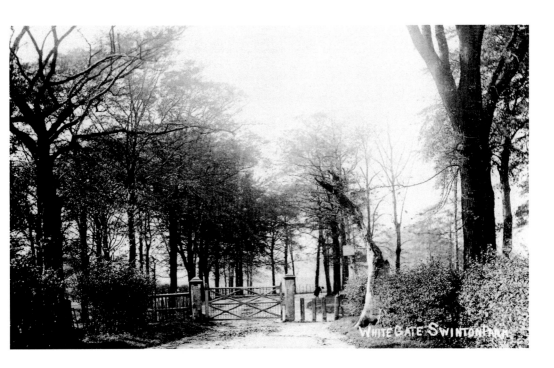

White Gate, Swinton Park, Manchester Road, 1908
A large area of Swinton in the nineteenth century consisted of Swinton Park, the grounds to Swinton House, at the park's northern end. There was an entrance drive from Manchester Road, past Harold Gate to Swinton House, which was set among woods and path systems, leading to a lake. Other paths, like the one above, ran to a separate dwelling on the park's western boundary. The house and other dwellings have now gone, with modern development south and west of Manchester Road.

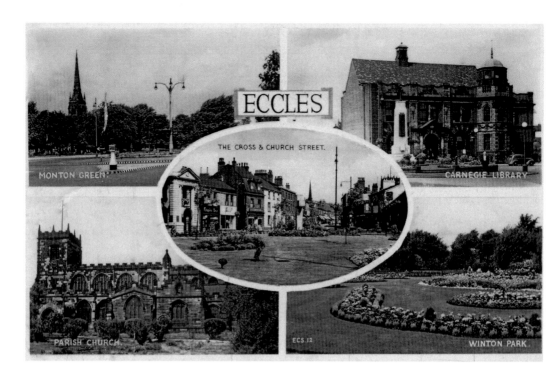

Monton Green, Carnegie Library, Eccles Cross and Church Street, St Mary's Church and Winton Park, *c.* 1960

This multi view postcard of Eccles includes a photograph of Winton Park, at Dover Street, Winton, which was first opened in 1906. The park has recently undergone a major refurbishment, including improvements to the bowling pavilion, and is the recipient of a Green Flag Award. Winton is located between Monton, Worsley, Peel Green and Patricroft, and the village is bisected by the motorway network, most notably the M60 and M602. Its name is derived from the original Anglo Saxon, meaning 'windy village.'

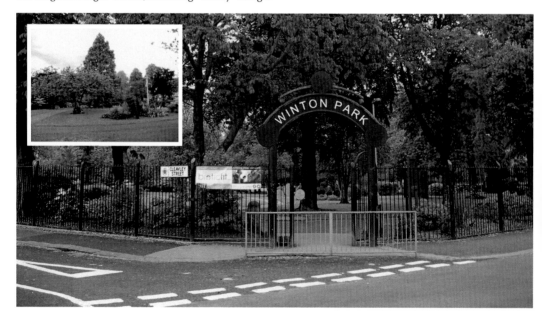

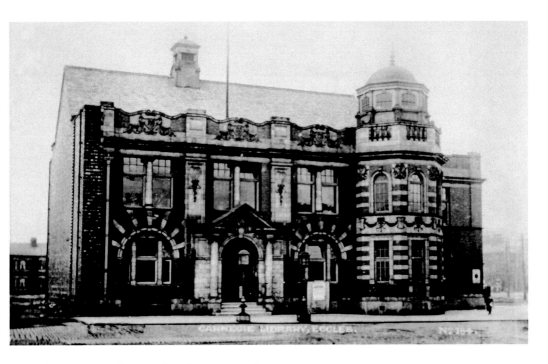

The Carnegie Library, Church Street, Eccles, c. 1907
Eccles Library was built on a slum clearance site in the town centre. It was funded by philanthropist Andrew Carnegie, who donated the construction costs of £7,500, and was designed by Edward Potts, opening on 19 October 1907. Built in the Renaissance style, it is Grade II listed. The Cenotaph opposite (inset) was erected in 1925, with a local sculptor, John Cassidy, commissioned to design it. Built of Portland stone, with a bronze figure, it was unveiled by Lord Derby, August 1925, and is Grade II listed.

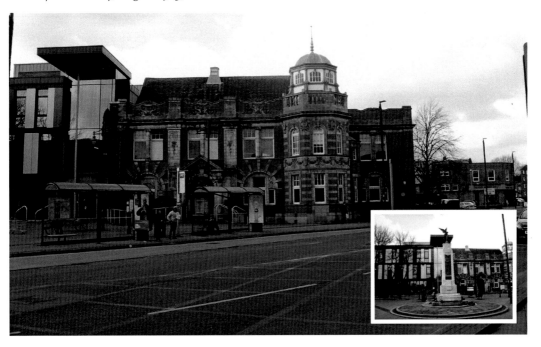

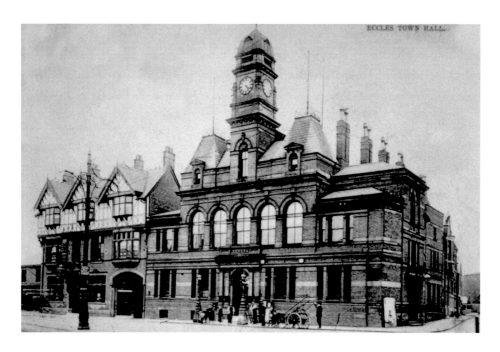

Town Hall, Church Street, Eccles, c. 1900

Built on the site of the old cockpit, replacing overcrowded rooms in Patricroft, the building opened on 3 November 1881 for the Local Board of Health. It then became the town hall when the Borough of Eccles was established in 1892. In 1889, the structure was extended at the back, providing police courts, a new council chamber and committee rooms. Then in 1974, Eccles was incorporated into Salford, with its headquarters at Swinton and the building lay empty. It is now utilised by the local community.

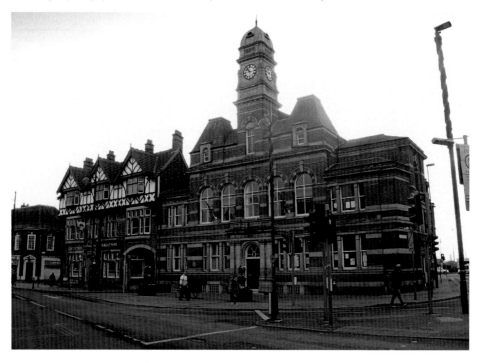

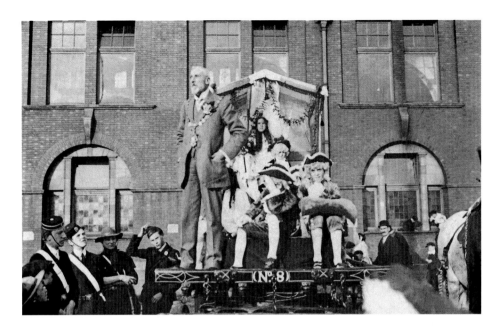

The Mayor of Eccles and Chain of Office, *c.* 1917, and Eccles Town Hall, the Mayor's HQ until 1974

The mayor's chain of office is now worn by the Ceremonial Mayor of Salford. It is of 15 carat gold and consists of twenty links incorporating the initials of former Mayors of the borough and the roses of Lancashire and Yorkshire. Weighing just under 1 kilogram, it is about 106 centimetres in length and is inscribed 'In commemoration of the sixtieth year of the reign of Queen Victoria presented by Councillor C. E. Hindley, Mayor 1895/6 and 1896/7'. An additional pendant was made in 1974.

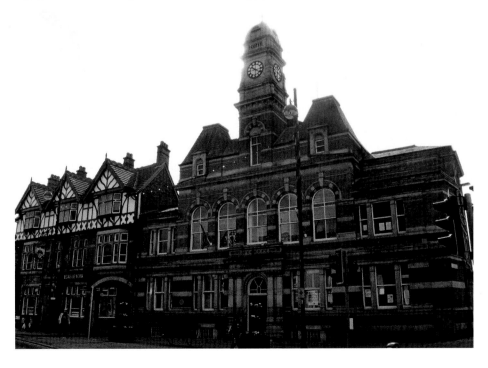

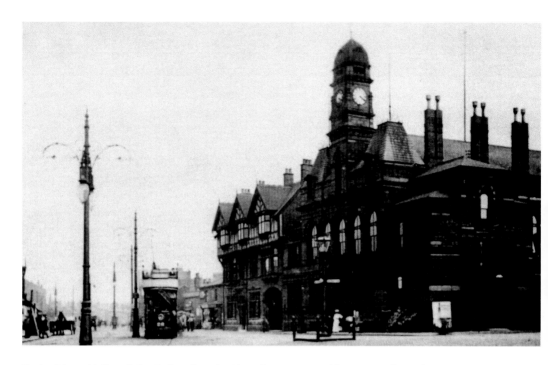

Eccles Town Hall and the Duke of York, Church Street, Looking Towards Eccles Cross, *c.* 1904
The Duke of York public house has held this name since 1794, with the old Eccles cockpit only reached by passing through the building. In July 1884, when alterations were being made, an old Manchester Mercury newspaper, dated 2 February 1796, was discovered, making it a place of historical importance. In the 1840s, the Duke of York was used by mail coaches on the journey from Manchester to Liverpool. Then in 1896, Adam Oldfield took over and rebuilt the business, which reopened in 1898.

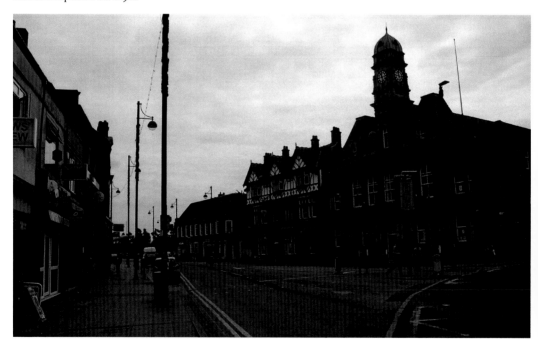

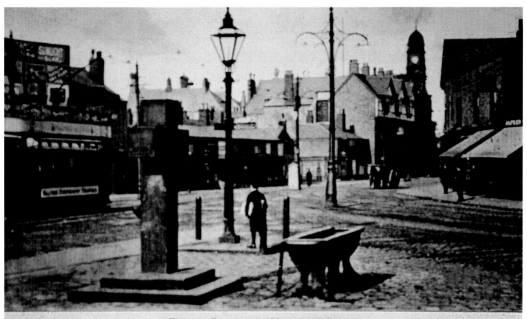

ECCLES CROSS AND MARKET PLACE.

Eccles Cross, Church Street, Looking Towards the Town Hall, *c.* 1910
The original Eccles Cross is shown in the centre of the above photograph, surrounded by cobbled roadways and an electric tram in the background. Next to the cross is a water trough, located here to provide refreshment for horses passing by. A horse and cart can be seen passing the town hall, clock tower and the Duke of York public house next to them. Today this view is dominated by the Metrolink and Bus Interchange, on the left of the modern image.

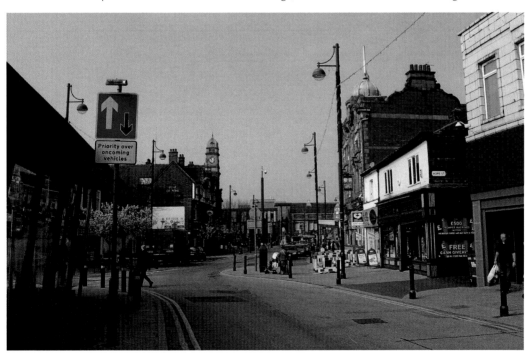

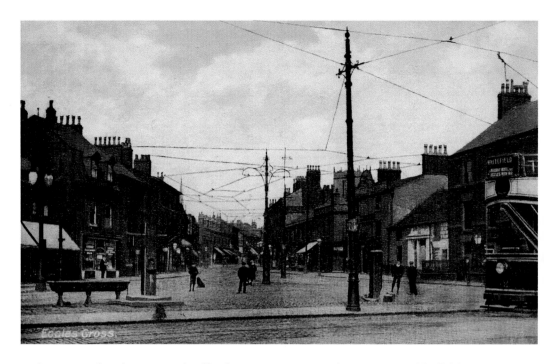

Eccles Cross, Church Street and Salford Tramways Corporation Tram to Whitefield, 1906
The Salford Corporation tram, shown above, has a destination of Whitefield, via Regent Road and Eccles New Road. Today trams still play an important part in transport links from Eccles to other areas of Salford and Manchester. The Metrolink Eccles line was approved in 1996, with the station built on Church Street/Regent Street junction, near to bus links and the railway station, on Church Street. The station opened for service on 21 July 2000 and officially by HRH the Princess Royal, January 2001.

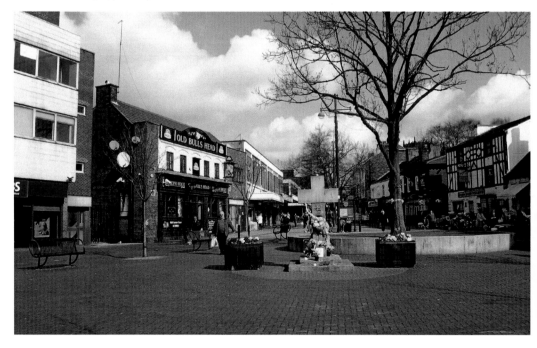

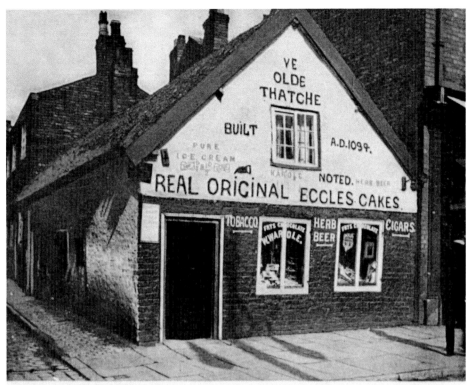

THE OLD ECCLES CAKE SHOP, Eccles.

The Vine eries.
No. 150.

'Ye Olde Thatche', the Old Eccles Cake Shop, Eccles Cross, Church Street, c. 1900
James Birch began making Eccles Cakes in a shop overlooking Eccles parish church in 1796. In 1810, he moved to larger premises opposite, which have since been used by various retail and commercial concerns. The original shop was taken over by James Bradburn, a former employee, who rebuilt the premises in 1835. There remained great rivalry between these establishments. Bradburn's shop was eventually demolished in the late 1960s for Eccles Shopping Precinct. 'Ye Olde Thatche' sold Eccles Cakes from its location opposite Eccles Cross.

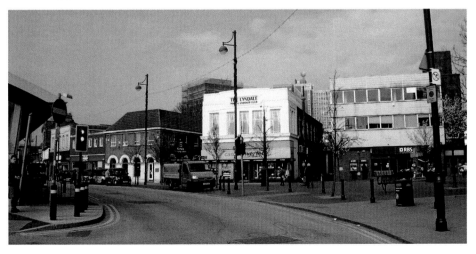

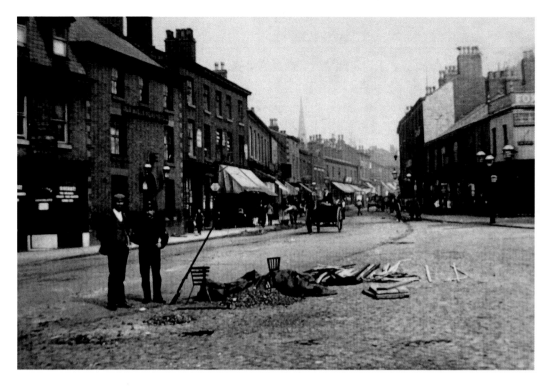

Church Street and the Old Bull's Head (left), Eccles, *c.* 1910
A workman and police constable pose on Church Street, where there is some road repair work being undertaken. In the background, the spire of Clarendon Road Congregational Church is visible, with the buildings in front of it, on Church Street, once the site of a graveyard. Located at the top of Church Street, beyond the parish church and opposite to the railway station, it was built as an overflow graveyard to house victims of several waves of cholera, which hit Eccles in the nineteenth century.

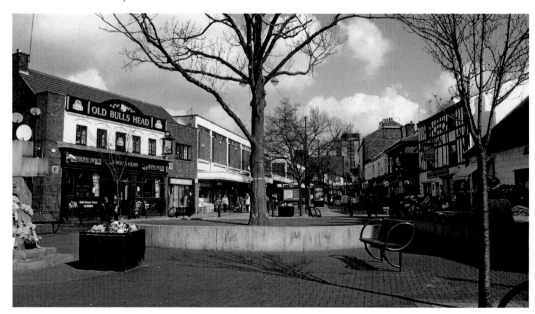

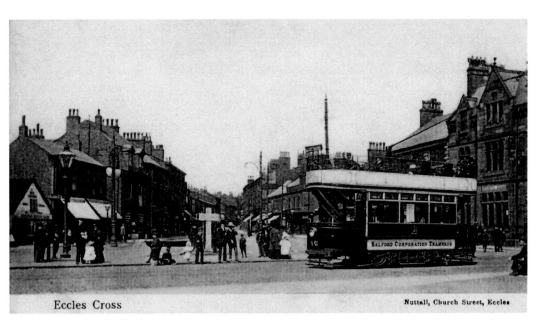

Eccles Cross

Nuttall, Church Street, Eccles

Church Street – Eccles Cross and Salford Tramways Corporation Tram, 1904, and Eccles Metrolink and Bus Interchange, 2015
The last tram in Salford ran on 31 March 1947, delayed from 1939 due to the outbreak of Second World War. In 1946, Salford Tramways Corporation became Salford City Transport, with the livery of its buses changing from red and white to green and cream, a situation that did not change until SELNEC assumed control on 1 November 1969. After this date, the livery of public transport across Salford and Greater Manchester became orange and white, until the early 1980s and 'privatisation.'

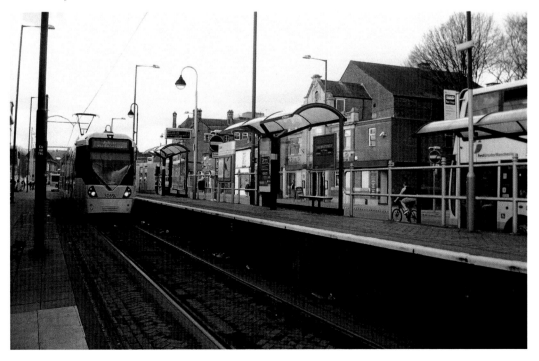

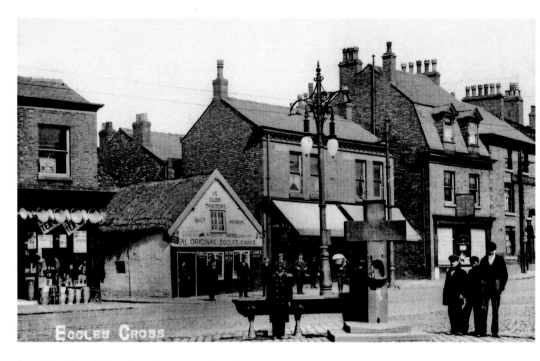

'Ye Olde Thatche' and Eccles Cross, Church Street, 1905
The original Eccles Cross was erected by Celtic missionaries in the fifth century. The carving of a later Saxon cross stood neglected for years, until accidentally demolished by a lorry on the first night of the blackout during the Second World War. After this incident, it was then put into storage for safe keeping but was somehow lost, with the present cross being a modern replica. Its location was next to the present cross, near the junction of Regent Street and Church Street.

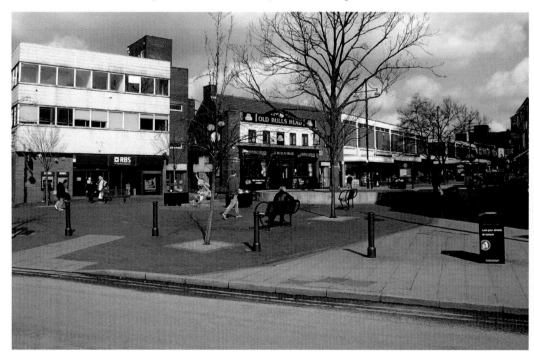

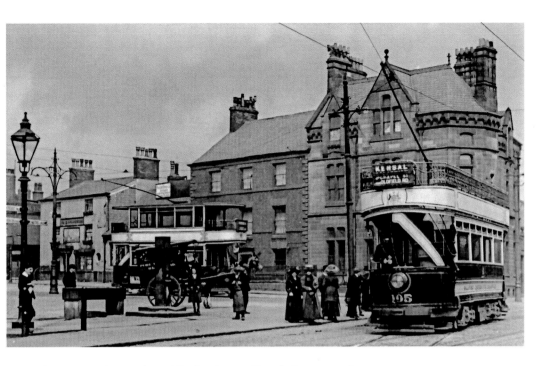

The Hare and Hounds and Eccles Cross, Church Street, 1906
Christianity and the first Eccles Cross arrived around the fifth century, becoming the site of a market (inset). There is evidence of prehistoric human settlement in the area, with dugout boats found at Barton-upon-Irwell and an arrowhead, spear and axes at Winton, suggesting a hunting and nomadic existence. Human occupation may extend as far back as 6000 BC. Agriculture predominated until the Industrial Revolution began *c.* 1750. The Hare and Hounds, to the left of the bank, and now a discount store, closed in 2008.

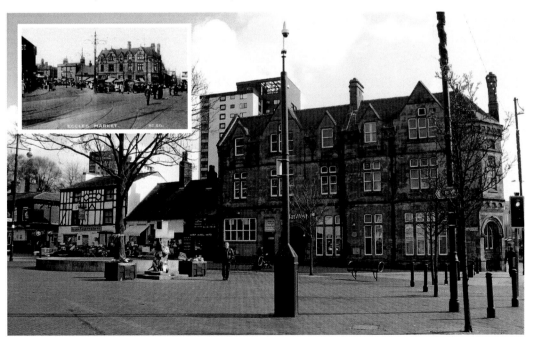

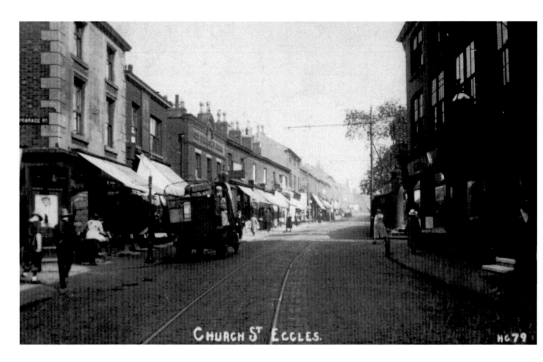

The Grapes (right) and Odd Fellows Arms (far left), Church Street, Eccles, c. 1910
Today the Odd Fellows Arms is a modern reconstruction of the original public house and still faces St Mary's parish church and its churchyard, as shown in the photograph of c. 1910. The cobblestone road has been replaced by twenty-first-century paving, in order to facilitate a safe environment for shoppers. There are no longer tramlines in the roadway, or motor traffic along Church Street; these have been replaced by telephone boxes, street lighting and café patrons enjoying their coffee.

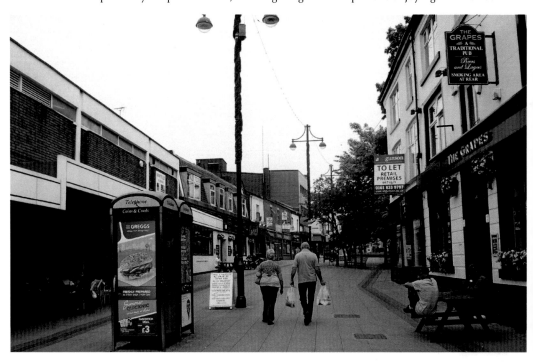

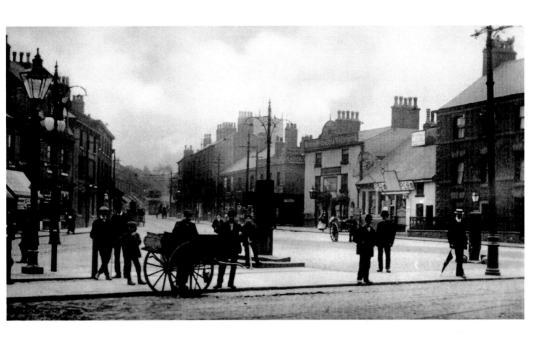

Eccles Cross, Church Street, 1912

In this photograph can be seen the Hare and Hounds public house – shown as a white building with three storeys, standing to the right side of Church Street. It closed as a licensed establishment in 2008. Directly opposite on the left stands the Old Bull's Head, built in 1893. Close by is the Eccles Cross public house (inset), formerly the Regent Cinema and Silver Screen nightclub, and just visible, next to the Hare and Hounds, is Finn M'Coul's public house, formerly the Fox Vaults.

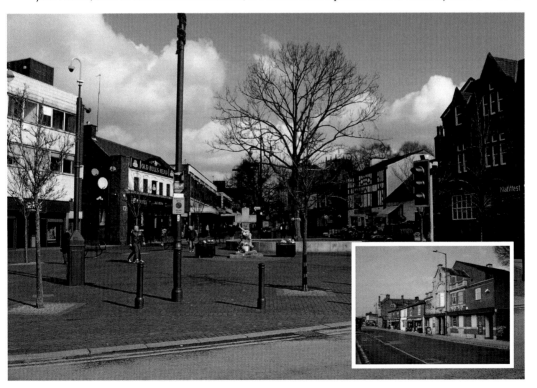

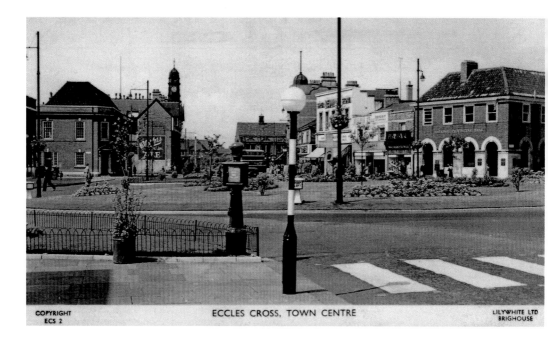

COPYRIGHT
ECS 2

ECCLES CROSS, TOWN CENTRE

LILYWHITE LTD
BRIGHOUSE

Eccles Cross and Church Street, from Regent Street, and inset, Broadway Cinema, to the left of Eccles Cross, c. 1950

By the mid-twentieth century, we can see that the area around Eccles Cross, where the junctions of Church Street and Regent Street intersect, has further changed. The above photograph shows a large roundabout, decorated with floral displays, and a 'zebra crossing,' designed for the management of motor vehicles. By the early twenty-first century, the emphasis has changed to the use of public transport, with the area dominated by the Metrolink and Bus Interchange on the left of the modern photograph.

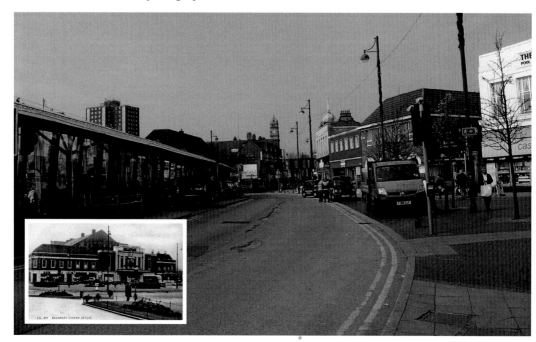

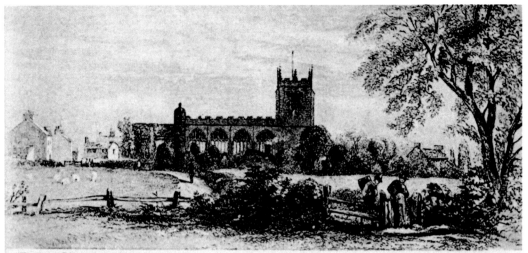

Eccles Church, 100 years ago.

Nuttall, Church Street, Eccles.

Eccles Parish Church 'One Hundred Years Ago,' *c.* 1800

It is thought that the district around the parish church possibly came to be known as Eccles, from the Latin 'ecclesia,' meaning 'church'. The building of the church took place *c.* 1100, although the earliest reference to it dates from 1120. There have been many alterations since 1769, when the north and south galleries were erected. These include the east gallery, built in 1805, with a new roof placed over the galleries in 1852, and in 1855, the old flagstone floor was removed (inset, interior, *c.* 1910).

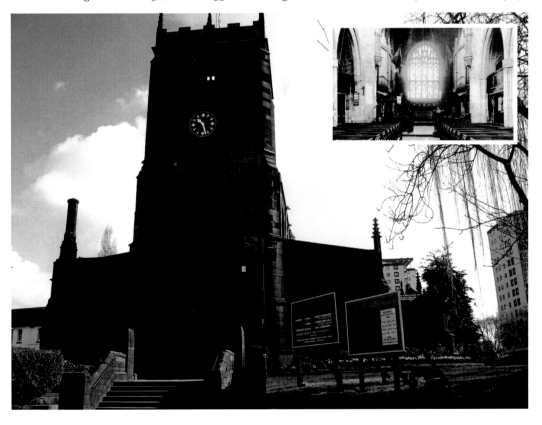

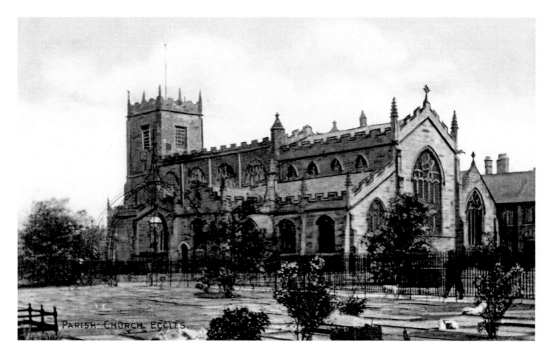

Eccles Parish Church and Churchyard, Church Street, 1905

The Victorian era saw continued development of Eccles parish church. In 1855, the old oak pulpit, which had been encased in deal, was restored to its original condition, and in 1862, there were several further alterations. The eastern gallery was removed, the old vestry at the west end was converted into the main entrance, the old organ built in 1813 was replaced by a more modern one, the Brereton tomb was moved, and a new roof was erected over the chancel.

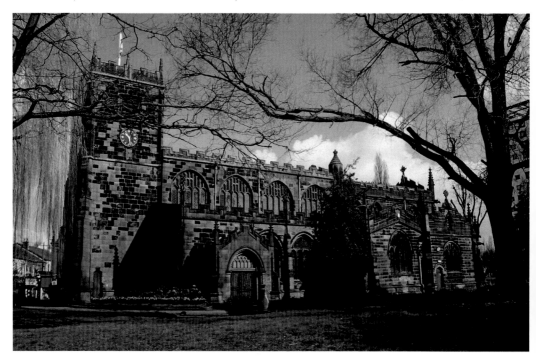

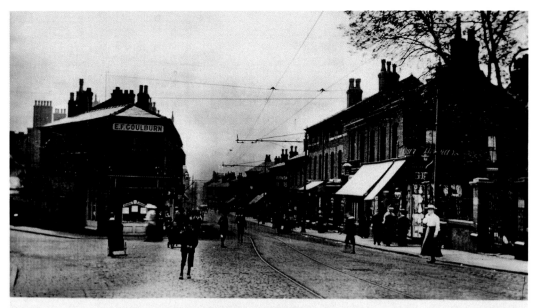

CHURCH STREET. ECCLES.

Church Street, Eccles, 1916

Church Street was the main shopping district of Eccles at this time. This view looks towards Church Road's junction with Church Street on the left, where St Mary's parish church and vicarage (obscured from view by shops) are located. Behind the photographer is Eccles railway station, with the camera looking towards Eccles Cross and Market Place in the distance. St Mary's parish church, founded c. 1100 and first mentioned in 1120, is one of the most ancient in the area.

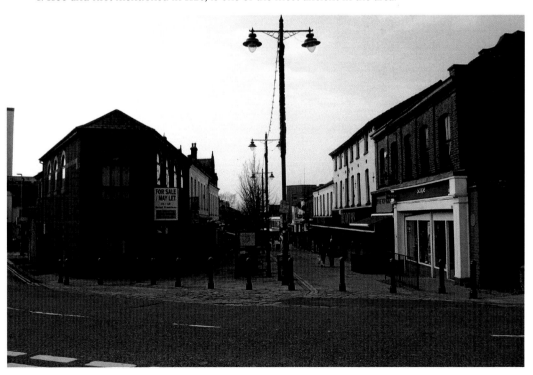

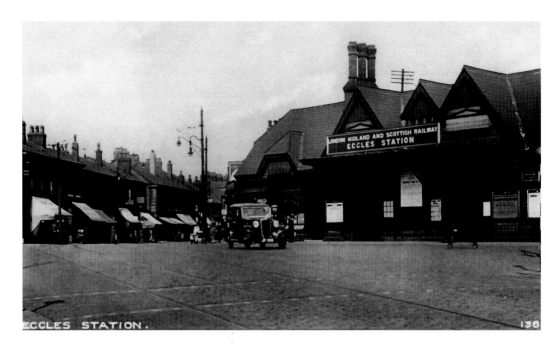

Eccles Railway Station, Church Street, *c.* 1930 and (inset) Platform Looking Towards Patricroft, 2015

Opened on 15 September 1830, the Liverpool and Manchester line was the world's first passenger railway and the scene of the first railway fatality in British history. Politician William Huskisson (1770–1830) was killed at Parkside station, when he fell under the wheels of Stephenson's Rocket while attending the opening ceremony. He was taken by train to Eccles and treated at the infirmary, where he was given laudanum. Realising his condition was hopeless, he was removed to Eccles vicarage, home of the Revd Thomas Blackburne, where he died.

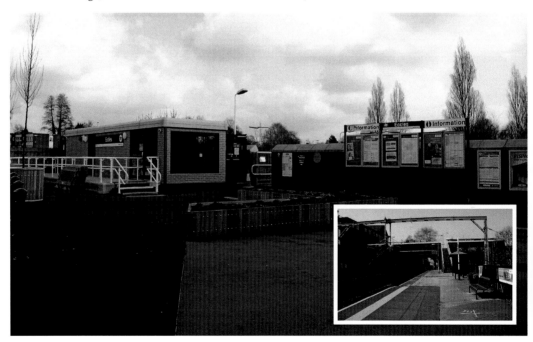

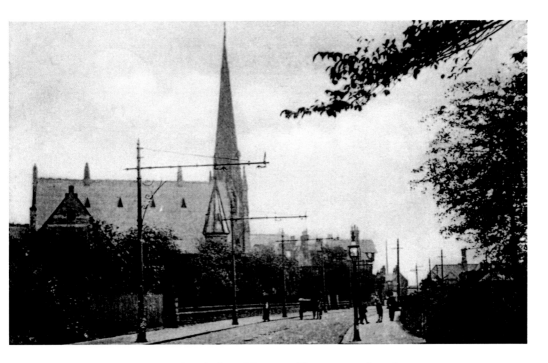

Clarendon Road Congregational Chapel from Wellington Road, Eccles, 1907
In this photograph, Eccles railway station is to the right of the photographer, who is looking along Wellington Road. Wellington Road's junction with Gilda Brook is beyond the church, to the left of the photographer. The railway runs along the right-hand side of the photograph, together with the M602 motorway today, meaning the buildings on the right are now gone, as is Clarendon Road Congregational Church and spire, founded in 1859 and today replaced by the United Reformed Church (left).

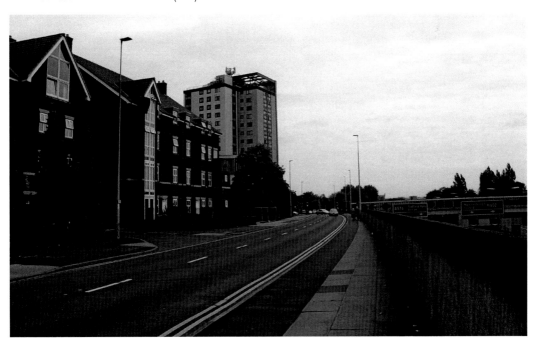

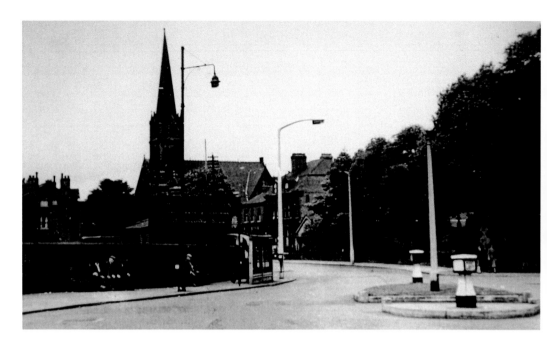

Immanuel Wesleyan Methodist Church, from the Junction of Wellington Road, Church Street and Clarendon Road *c.* 1960 and inset (foreground) from Wellington Road and Abbey Grove *c.* 1930
The Immanuel Wesleyan Methodist Church was founded in 1874 and closed in 1969, at the time when the M602 motorway was being constructed through the district. The church was without a graveyard. The Wesleyan Methodist Church was founded in the eighteenth century, from societies that originated through John Wesley and his preachers. By the nineteenth century it was the largest Nonconformist denomination. In 1932, together with other independent denominations, it became the Methodist Church of Great Britain.

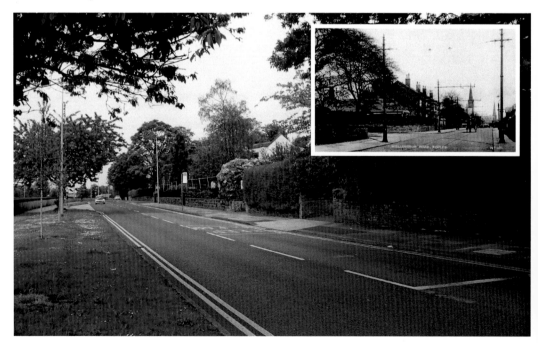

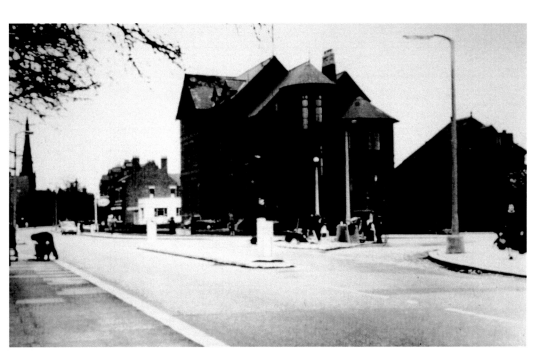

Eccles Liberal Club, Junction of Wellington Road and Albert Street, *c*. 1960
Built in 1890, today the Liberal Club is still located on Wellington Road in a new building, at its junction with Albert Road opposite (inset, right). This photograph looks along Wellington Road, towards the railway station and the spire of the Wesleyan Methodist Church, now demolished. The area has changed radically since the construction of the M602 motorway, *c*. 1970 (inset, left), which runs behind the demolished Liberal Club. Properties were compulsorily purchased, with Albert Street now Albert Road Bridge (inset, looking towards Patricroft).

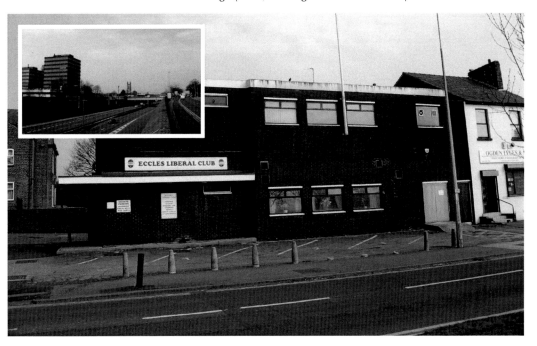

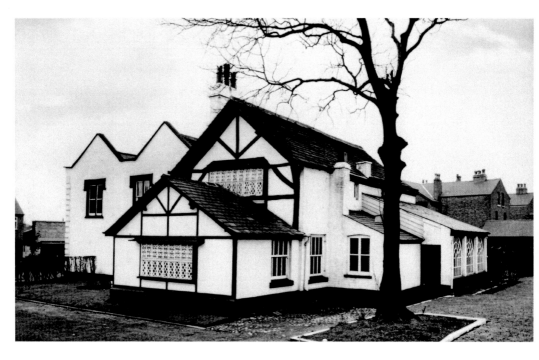

Monk's Hall Museum, Junction of Wellington Road and Monk's Hall Grove, Eccles, c. 1961
Originating from c. 1200, it is a Tudor residence with modern additions. The monks of Whalley
Abbey were landowners in Eccles from the 1230s, and Henry de Monks lived in Eccles c. 1394,
either could have given the hall its name. In the 'Monk's Hall Hoard', six thousand medieval
coins were discovered when a new road was being constructed in 1864. Monk's Hall was
purchased by Eccles Council in 1959 and opened as a museum in 6 July 1961, closing in the late
1980s. It now lies derelict.

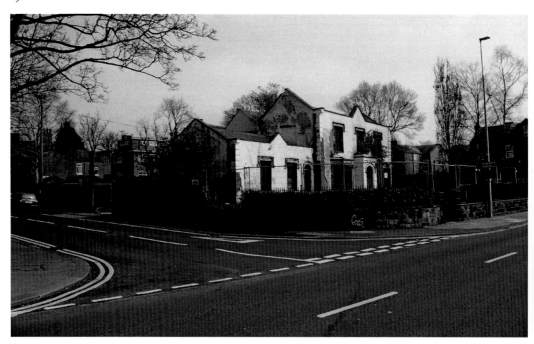

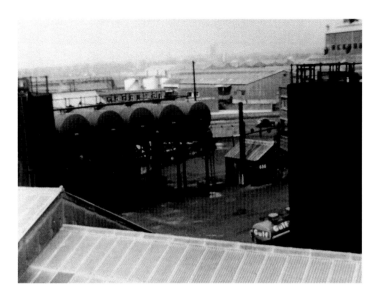

St Andrew's Parish Church, Chadwick Road, Eccles, from Gulf Oil, Trafford Park, 1960, and from Wellington Road, 2015

St Andrew's opened in 1879 to a design by Henry Tijon, with the tower built in 1889. The church originally had little interior decoration – later added over the years. Today the building is Grade II listed, with many additional architectural features. Four months after the church was consecrated, a church school was opened, later St Andrew's Primary School, the present building on Oxford Street dating from 1893. A second school in Monton, which was then part of the parish, opened in 1881.

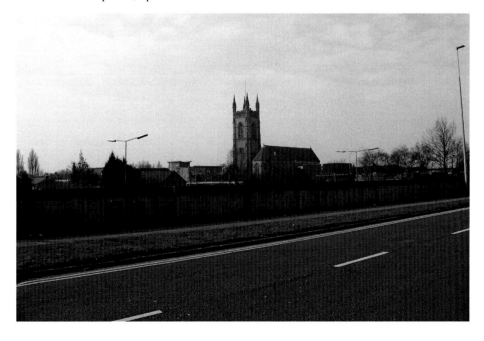

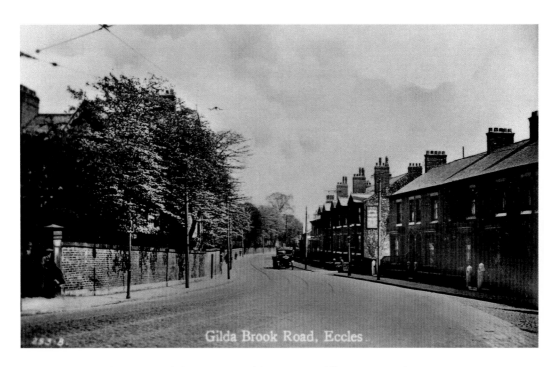

Gilda Brook Road *c.* 1930 and the Former White Horse Public House, Eccles, 2015
Named after nearby Gilda Brook, which is belowground and inaccessible for much of its course. Formerly Broom House Lane, in 1803, there was an inn here called the Shovel and Broom, later renamed the Trafford Volunteer in 1809 and the Volunteer in 1810. In 1825, it was again renamed, becoming the White Horse, and was rebuilt in 1929, reopening 1935. Demolished in 1969, it was rebuilt in 1973 and is now a retail outlet. It was once owned by Beverley Callard of Coronation Street fame.

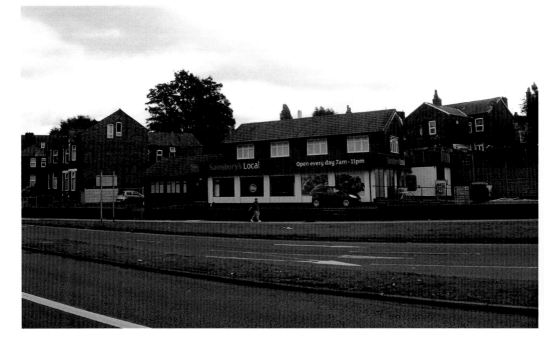

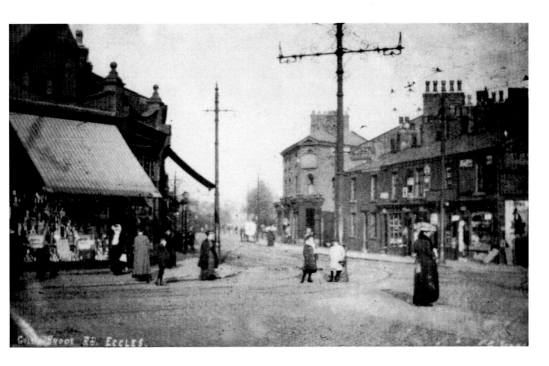

Gilda Brook Road, Eccles, c. 1910

The original Gilda Brook Road bears little resemblance to its modern counterpart. It takes traffic off the M602 motorway, providing a link route onto Eccles Old Road and past Salford Royal Hospital, heading towards the City of Salford. In the first decade of the twentieth century, trams were the main form of public transport, with their tracks clearly seen on Gilda Brook Road. Also shown are Edwardian pedestrians, crossing the road to take advantage of the many retail outlets, once located here.

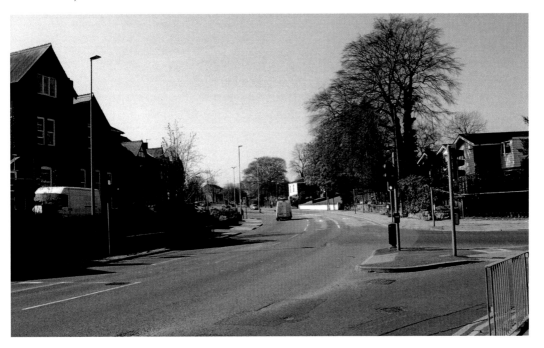

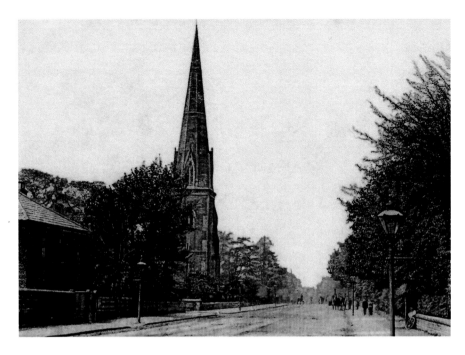

Eccles Old Road and Hope Parish Church, St James, 1894
The church is located at the western end of Pendleton, has a boundary with the parish of St Mary, Eccles, and is included because it is a landmark church located on one of the traditional ancient routes into Eccles – Eccles Old Road. It is also close to Salford's famous teaching hospital, Salford Royal, formerly Hope Hospital. The church was consecrated on 14 December 1861. It reputedly has the highest concentration of Capronnier stained-glass windows in a single location.

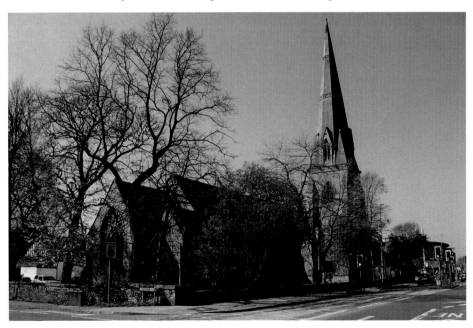

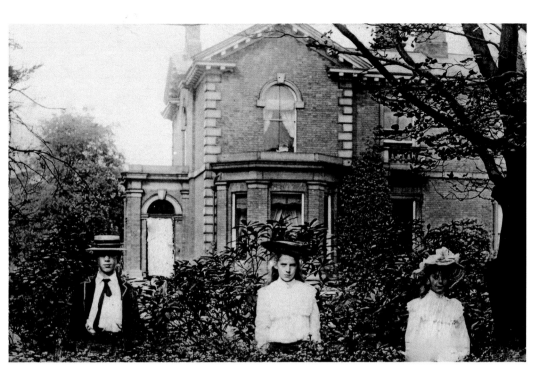

The Blakeley Family, No. 14 Preston Avenue, Eccles, 1904
No. 14 Preston Avenue borders onto the Ellesmere Park Conservation Area and is a typical property of the late Victorian/Edwardian eras. Within the area, over 75 per cent of the houses were built in this period. They are typically two- or three-storied, detached or semi-detached residences and are of generous proportions, being set in large grounds, giving plenty of space between neighbouring residences. They 'possess a strong vertical emphasis in design', as shown in the photograph above.

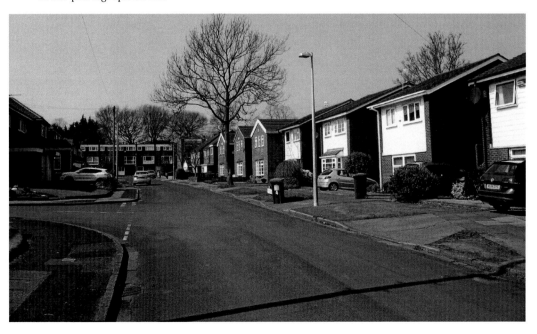

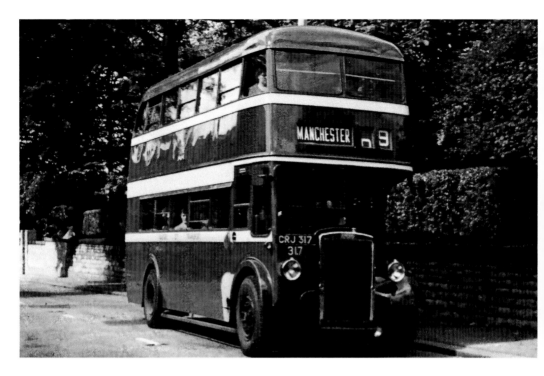

Salford City Transport Daimler Bus, at Half Edge Lane, Eccles, 1958
Registration No. CRJ 317 has a destination of Manchester, with this service terminating at Victoria Bus Station. Despite the fact that it was in Salford, the bus station was the nearest stop to the City of Manchester. Between 1950 and 1952, Salford City Transport placed in service 195 Daimler CVG6 double-decker buses, with Metro-Cammell Phoenix bodies. For ten years, they were the 'backbone' of the city's fleet. On 1 November 1969, SELNEC took over possession of the surviving Daimler buses.

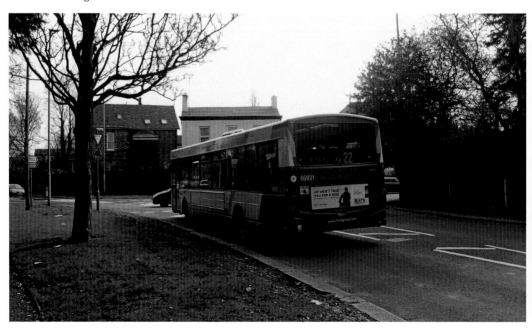

Eccles Masonic Lodge, Half Edge Lane, c. 1921

The Eccles and District Group of Lodges meet in two Masonic Halls at Eccles (Half Edge Lane) and Swinton (Border Lodge), both in the Metropolitan Borough of Salford. Eccles Masonic Hall was originally a private house built in 1846, called Elm Bank, which was used as a convalescent home in the First World War, and then purchased in 1921 by seven Eccles lodges. It is now home to twelve lodges, with Ecclesholme, a retirement home built in 1973 on adjacent land, maintaining very close links.

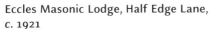

Chas. Goddard. PATRICROFT.

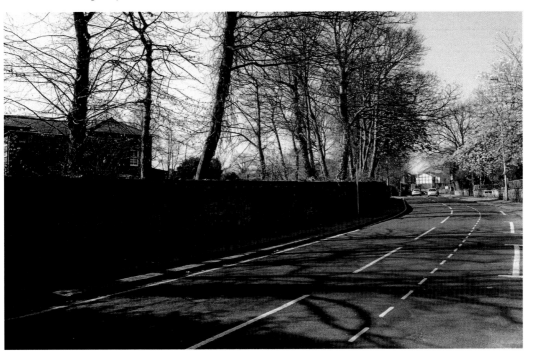

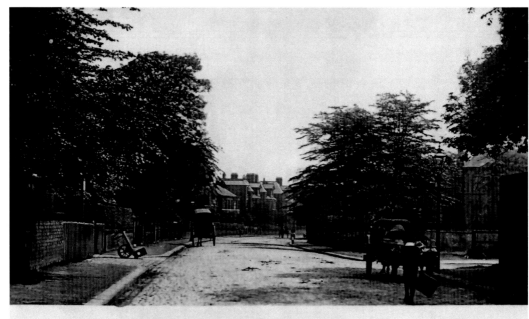

VICTORIA CRESCENT, ECCLES.

Victoria Crescent, Eccles, 1913

Close to the Ellesmere Park Conservation Area, Victoria Crescent, as well as some adjacent roads, has seen some later residential developments – mainly in the interwar and post-war periods. There has been a certain amount of 'infill' between the larger Victorian/Edwardian properties, together with some isolated examples of the redevelopment of cleared sites, adding to the character of the older development. Like other roads in the vicinity, many residences on Victoria Crescent are particularly fine examples of their period.

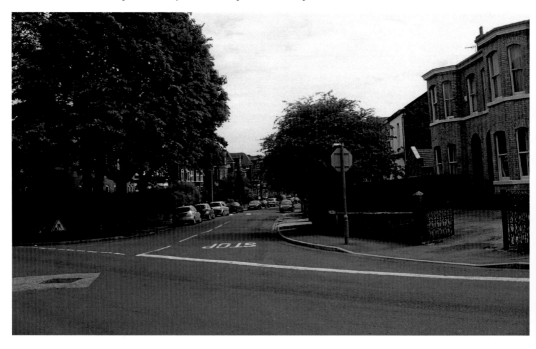

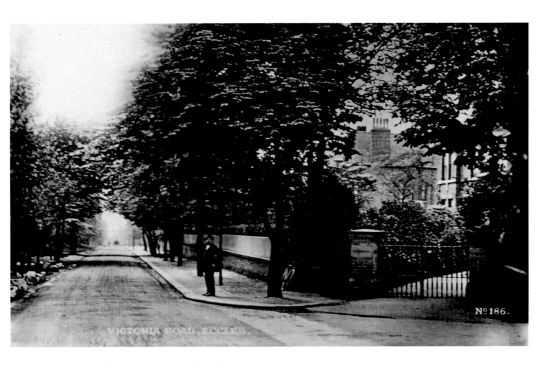

Victoria Road, Ellesmere Park, Eccles, 1923

Victoria Road is photographed here at its junction with Sandwich Road – its junction with Half Edge Lane is behind the photographer. This view has changed very little since the original one was taken in 1923. Now, Victoria Road is a part of the Ellesmere Park Conservation Area and retains its authentic-looking gas lamps, adapted for modern electric lighting. The road, like most in the Conservation Area, continues to be tree-lined and remains, quiet, residential and essentially Victorian/Edwardian in character.

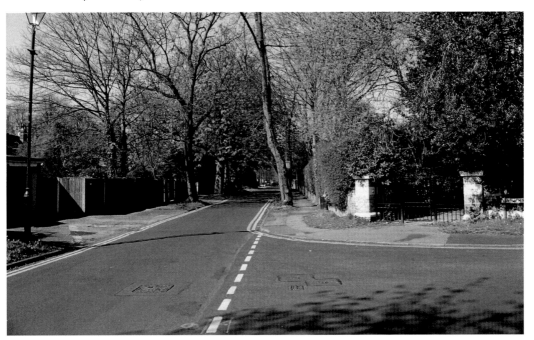

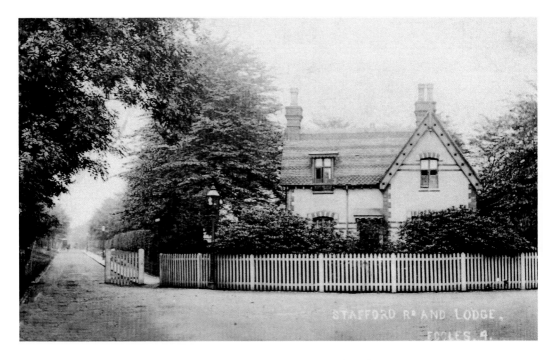

Stafford Road and Lodge, Ellesmere Park, from Monton Road, Eccles, 1904
Like many of the roads on exclusive Victorian/Edwardian housing estates, Stafford Road was protected from the main Monton Road by gates and a substantial lodge at its entrance. This photograph of Stafford Road looks towards the Three Sisters (Ellesmere Park), now designated a Local Nature Reserve. Salford Council enforces strict planning restrictions on the Conservation Area, and there is an active residents' association, working in conjunction with the local council to ensure planning applications to maintain continuity and consistency.

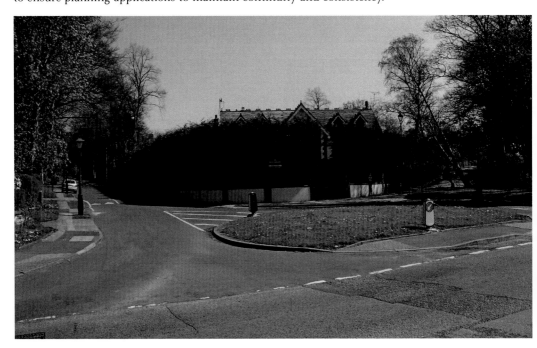

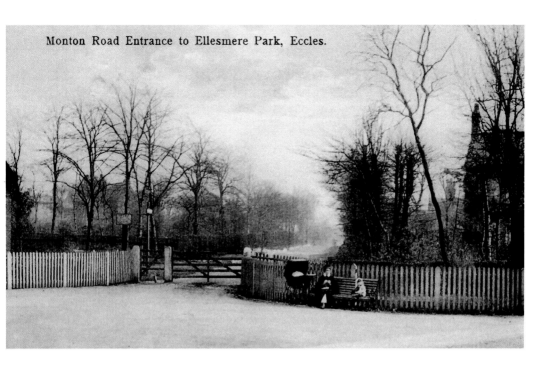

Monton Road Entrance to Ellesmere Park, Eccles.

Monton Road Entrance to Ellesmere Park, Eccles, c. 1900

In this view of the entrance to Ellesmere Park, as seen from Monton Road, Stafford Road and its entrance gate are clearly visible. The main difference is the size and growth of the surrounding trees, which are substantially larger in the modern image, with some recent replanting. The original lodge has been replaced by a newer and larger development, and the road in front of Stafford Road's junction with Victoria Road has been reconfigured to allow the safe passage of motor traffic.

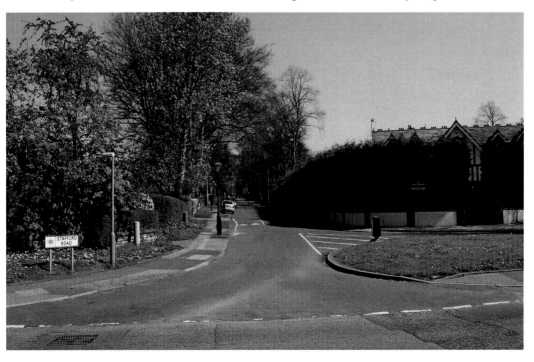

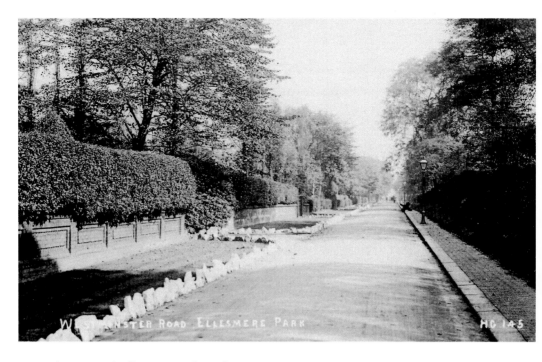

Westminster Road, Ellesmere Park, Eccles, 1908
Located in the 'Ellesmere Park Conservation Area', this photograph of Westminster Road has the name of one of the residences written in the corner and located by a cross on the photograph. 'Rowsley' (inset), built in 1903, stood in its own grounds in 1908 and is fairly typical of Ellesmere Park, characterising this district of Eccles as one of late nineteenth- and early twentieth-century properties, which provided an atmosphere of spaciousness and grandeur. Now residential, the property was once a nursing home.

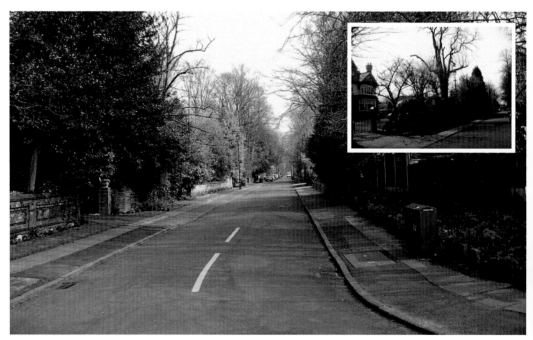

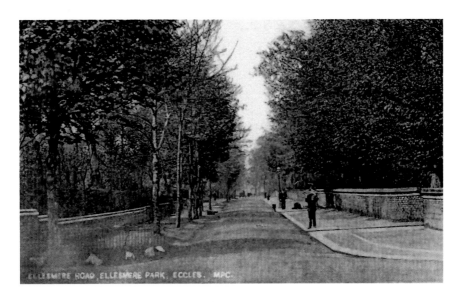

Ellesmere Road, Ellesmere Park, Eccles, 1894

In addition to the grandeur of the properties in the Ellesmere Park Conservation Area, it is characterised by the use of brick and stone walls in order to enclose the properties and form their boundaries. Most have long front gardens and benefit from wide, straight roads following a grid pattern, as shown in the photograph above. There are large numbers of mature trees favoured by the Victorians and creating avenues of foliage lining the highway, as at Ellesmere Road.

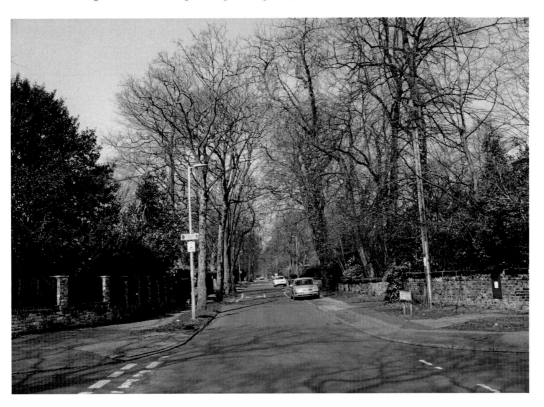

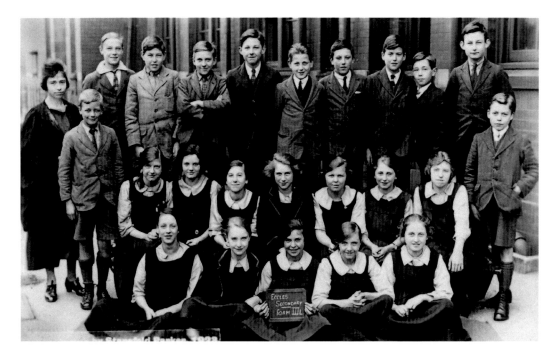

Eccles Secondary School, Form III L, Park Road, Monton, 1923, and Wentworth High School, Chatsworth Road, Ellesmere Park, 2015

Eccles Secondary school stood close to the site of Monton Grange and was the first secondary school built by Lancashire County Council after the 1902 Education Act. The foundation stone was laid by county education committee chairman, County Ald. Sir Henry Fleming Herbert, in 1910, with the first intake of pupils on 18 September 1911. In 1944, the school changed its name to Eccles Grammar School and in 1973 combined with Ellesmere Park Secondary School to become Ellesmere Park High School (Wentworth High School).

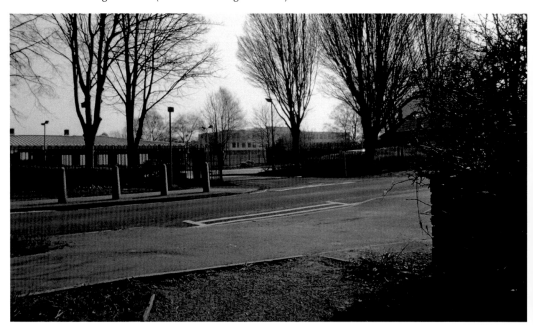

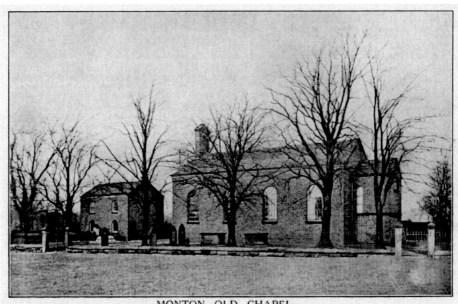

Photo by W. Barnes, Swinton. MONTON OLD CHAPEL.

Monton Old Chapel, Monton Green, *c.* 1860

When Nonconformist persecution was relaxed, services were held in a large barn at Monk's Hall. Later, the Act of Toleration saw the congregation purchase land (Greenfield), from Peter Ormerod, and the first Monton chapel was built *c.* 1697. In 1715, the chapel was destroyed by a Jacobite mob and then rebuilt. In 1848, an infant day school was established, with chapel alterations in 1850 and walls and rails around the chapel yard in 1851. The Unitarian church replaced the chapel in 1873–75.

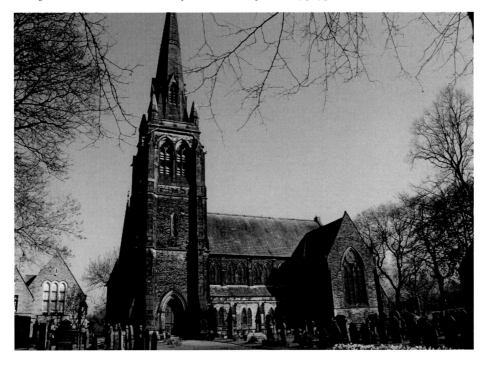

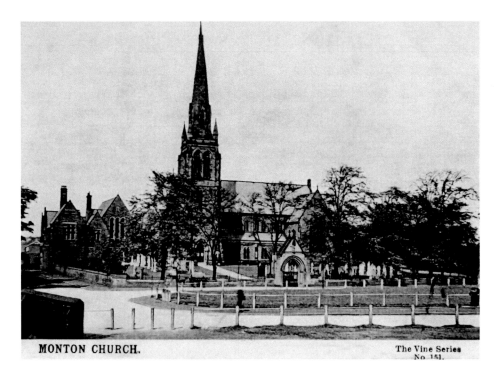

MONTON CHURCH.

The Vine Series
No. 151.

Monton Unitarian Church, Monton Green, c. 1900
Monton Unitarian church officially opened on 23 September 1875, although there have been other churches on the site since the seventeenth century. Other independent churches in the Monton area included the Eccles Wesleyans. In 1897, with a donation of £400 to the circuit, it was decided that because the district, its population and, therefore, the Eccles congregation had expanded so rapidly, a brick school and chapel should be built to serve Monton. This church, on Grange Drive (inset), opened on 27 January 1899.

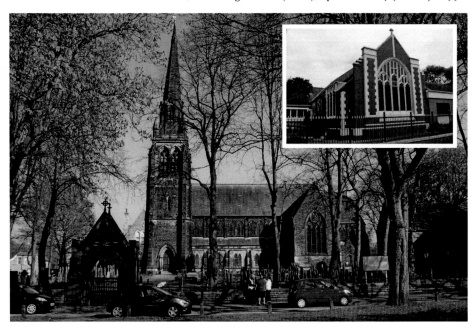

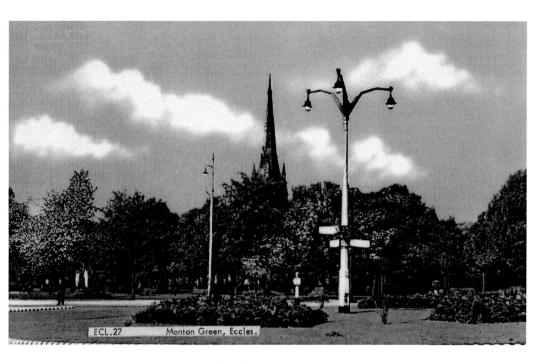

ECL.27   Monton Green, Eccles.

Monton Green and the Unitarian Church, Monton, c. 1950
Built from 1873 to 1875, the Grade II listed Unitarian church replaced Monton chapel, first established in 1697. The tower and steeple are separate from the main body of the church, as they were not part of the original plan, being constructed at a later date. The tower houses the bell from the old chapel, which was retained despite the offer of a peal of new bells. The lychgate is also Grade II listed and was erected in 1895, in memory of Henry Leigh.

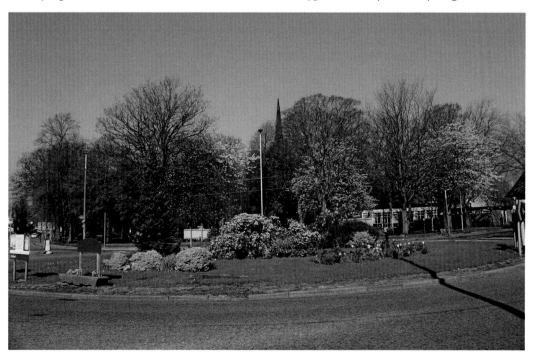

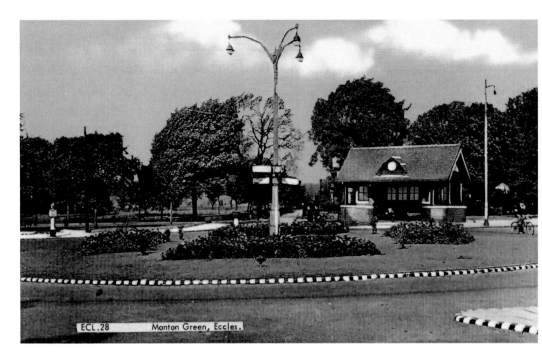

Monton Green, Looking Towards the Public Shelter, Monton, c. 1950
Monton Green became a Conservation Area in 1979, consisting of Monton Green and its public shelter, built in 1930 – the Grade II listed Unitarian church – and Grade II listed memorial schools (inset), with caretaker's house, designed by Thomas Worthington and J. G. Elgood, in 1888. Also included a lodge built in 1875 to the Earl of Ellesmere's former estate and Boddan Lodge and bowling green. Monton Green, used as common land until 1895, was conveyed to Eccles Corporation, who then undertook to maintain its public rights of way.

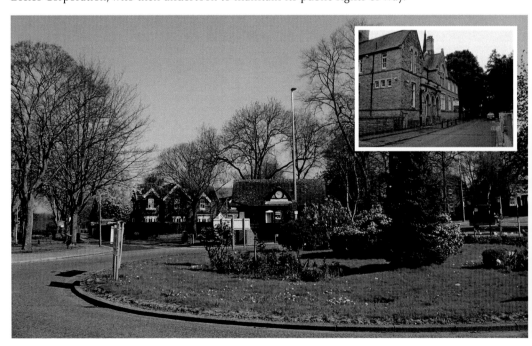

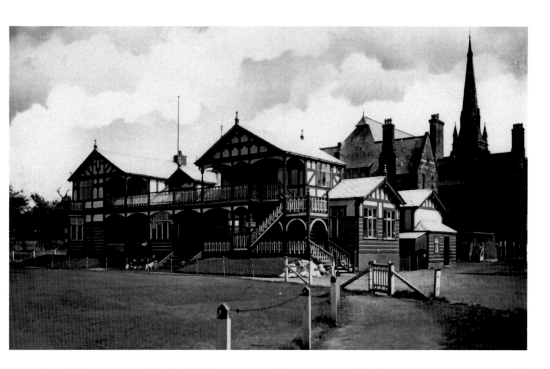

The Club House, Worsley Golf Club, _c._ 1923, and Former Caretaker's House to Monton Memorial Schools (Left) 2015, Stableford Avenue, Monton

The club was founded in 1894 by local businessman H. Stafford Golland. A site for the course at Broadoak Park, part of the Earl of Ellesmere's estate, was developed, with the Earl later becoming club president. The greens were completed at a cost of £20 15s 8d, with the first match taking place on 28 April 1894. In 1895, the club acquired its first pavilion, which was replaced by a new club house in April 1897, costing £1,300. This was extended substantially in 1923.

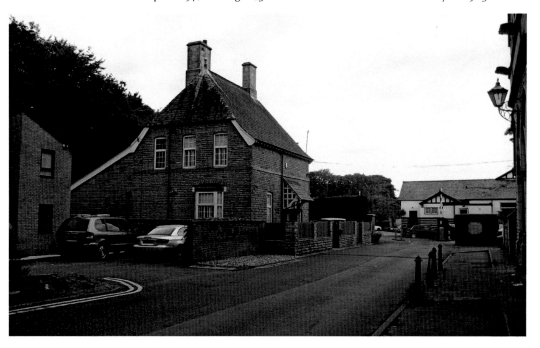

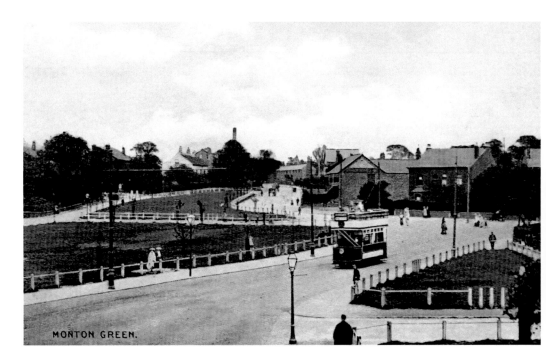

MONTON GREEN.

Monton Green, Looking Towards Eccles, 1910, and (inset) the Railway Station site and Bridgewater Canal, 2015

Monton Green railway station was originally a part of the Tyldesley Loop line, linking Eccles, Worsley, Leigh and Roe Green. The station opened on 1 November 1887 and was closed as part of the Beeching proposals on 5 May 1969. It was located on an embankment just off Monton Green, near a former colliery, the railway line running parallel to the Bridgewater Canal. The embankment upon which the station once stood now forms the starting point for a public pathway, run by Salford City Council.

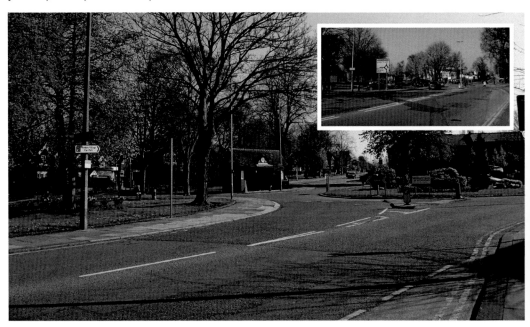

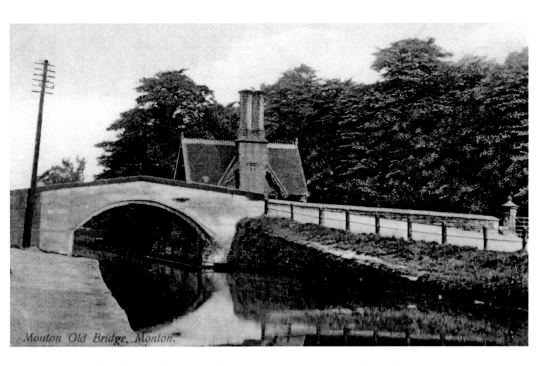
Monton Old Bridge, Monton.

Monton Old Bridge, Bridgewater Canal, Monton, Constructed c. 1760

The Bridgewater Canal was constructed by engineer James Brindley (1716–72), under the auspices of the Duke of Bridgewater, beginning in 1759 and opening on 17 July 1761. The 'Duke's Cut' supplied coal to the mills and factories of Manchester in an efficient, plentiful and economic manner, enabling the market town to become an industrial powerhouse of the nineteenth century and a major city. It replaced the packhorse transports, which had previously supplied goods along some notoriously dilapidated roads, with a more reliable and regular service.

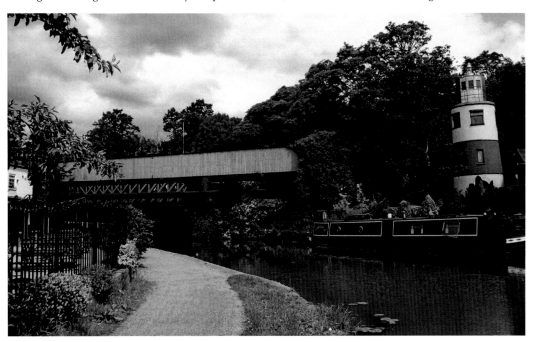

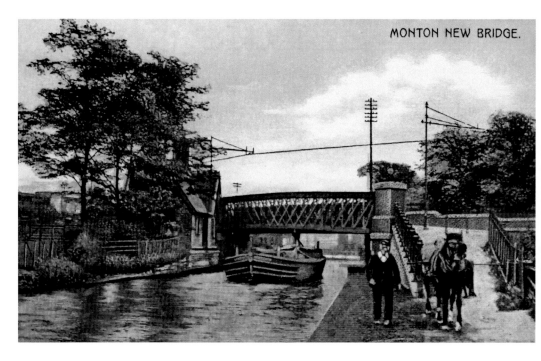

Monton New Bridge, Bridgewater Canal, Monton, *c.* 1910

The Bridgewater Canal was originally under the ownership of the Bridgewater Navigation Co. By 1885, it passed into the ownership of the Manchester Ship Canal Co., for the sum of £1,710,000. Monton New Bridge is shown here *c.* 1910, an iron structure installed to carry a tramway. Commercial traffic continued to be carried until 1974, with the canal still owned today by the Manchester Ship Canal Co. and the Bridgewater Canal Trust. Now, it is used mainly for leisure purposes.

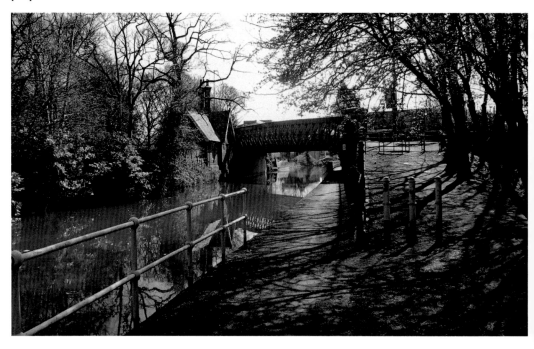

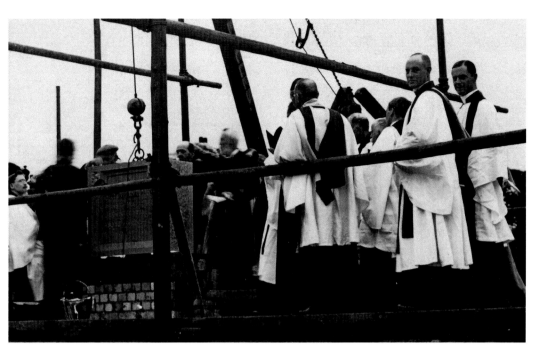

Laying of St Paul's Church Foundation Stone (inset), Egerton Road, Monton, 1907
The Anglican Church in Monton is dedicated to St Paul the Apostle and opened in 1908. It is located on Egerton Road. The land on which St Paul's Church and vicarage stand was originally part of a small farmstead known as Chestnut Cottage. An old barn on the site of Nasmyth's works was used for services, seating between seventy to eighty people and served by a curate from Eccles parish church. After 1868, Christ Church, Patricroft, served the district until St Paul's was constructed.

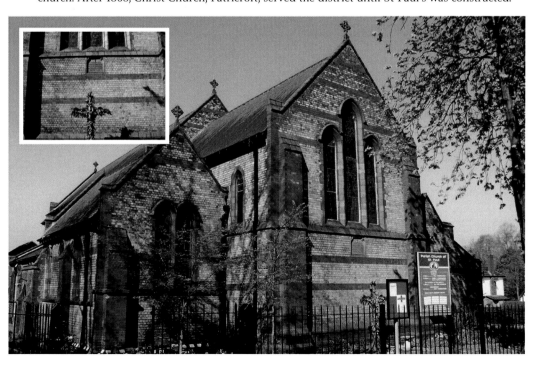

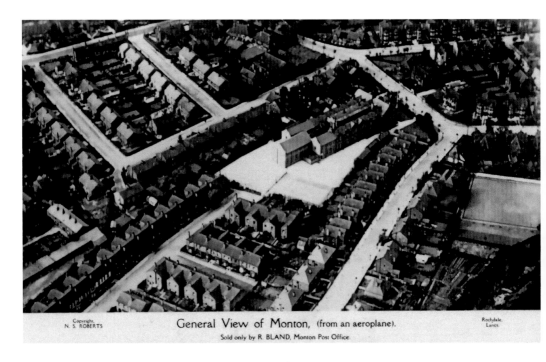

Copyright.
N. S. ROBERTS

General View of Monton, (from an aeroplane).

Rochdale.
Lancs.

Sold only by R. BLAND, Monton Post Office.

Aerial view of Eccles Secondary School, Park Road, Monton, c. 1930
Park Road runs along the front of Eccles Secondary School (centre), while Hawthorn Avenue runs along the right-hand side of the school, to a junction with Park Road, and Grange Drive runs along the left-hand side of the school, to junctions with Park Road and Monton Green. The site of the former school (inset, foundation stone) is now occupied by Old School Court. Bottom right is a bowling green and the now defunct Clifton branch railway line of the L&NWR.

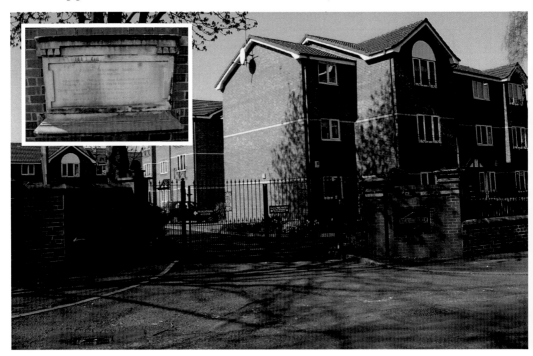

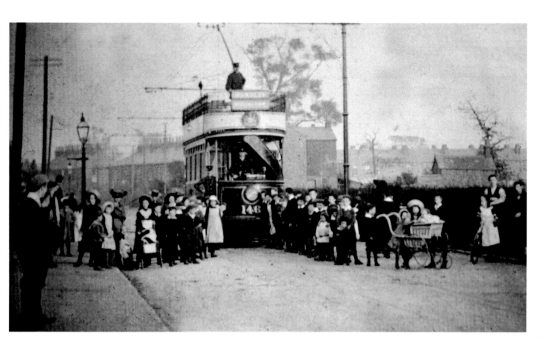

First Tram at Winton, *c.* 1905, and Eccles Metrolink and Bus Interchange, from Church Street, 2015

Salford City Transport began operating on 2 May 1901 as Salford (Tramways) Corporation, running horse-drawn tram cars in red and white livery, on tram lines purchased from neighbouring Manchester. By September 1901, the Corporation's first tram cars were delivered and put into service, operating from a depot and works located on Frederick Road. By July 1920, the Corporation's first motor buses were being purchased for a fleet that operated from a new depot in Weaste, recently constructed as their base.

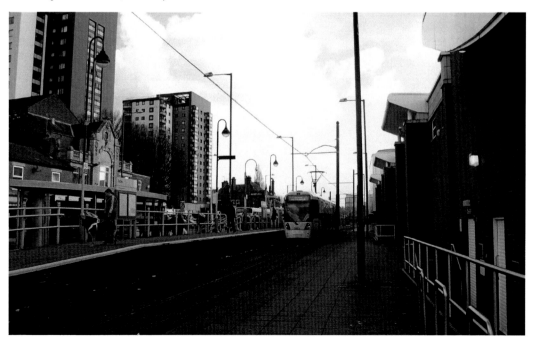

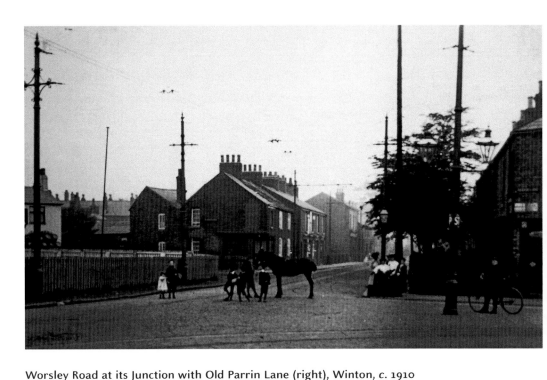

Worsley Road at its Junction with Old Parrin Lane (right), Winton, c. 1910
Worsley Road's junction with Old Parrin Lane has changed beyond all recognition since this photograph of *c.* 1910 was taken. Today the M602 motorway crosses at this point, with Old Parrin Lane running alongside the boundary of the M602 motorway, at Winton to the south, and Parrin Lane joining Worsley Road, on the northern side of the M602 motorway. The Brown Cow public house, which recently announced its closure, is just off camera on the left of Worsley Road.

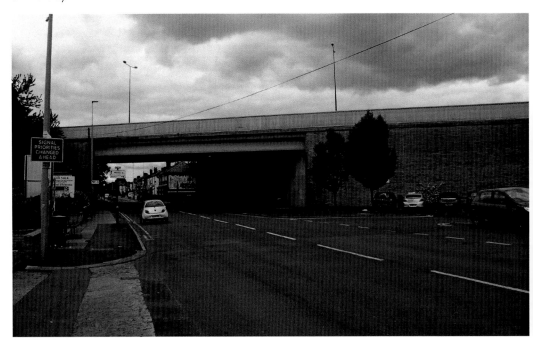

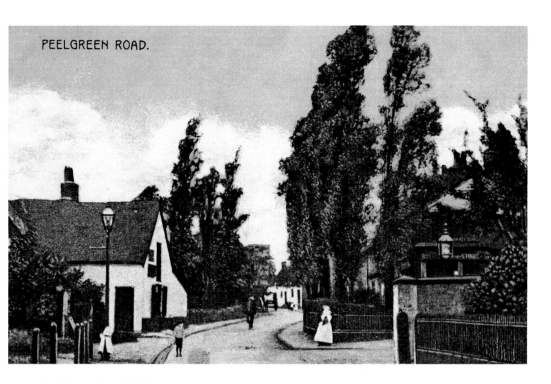

PEELGREEN ROAD.

Peel Green Road, Eccles, *c.* 1910

Peel Green forms part of the western end of the town of Eccles. The district is today split by the M60 motorway, which runs north–south through its centre. Until the recession of the 1980s, Peel Green was dominated by heavy industry, with Gardner's engine makers on Hardy Street and the Regent Tyre and Rubber Co., at the Enterprise Works on the corner of Green Street and Clifford Street, which are now both closed. It was once the terminus for local trams.

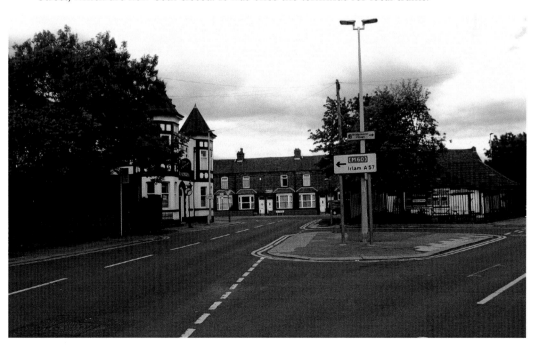

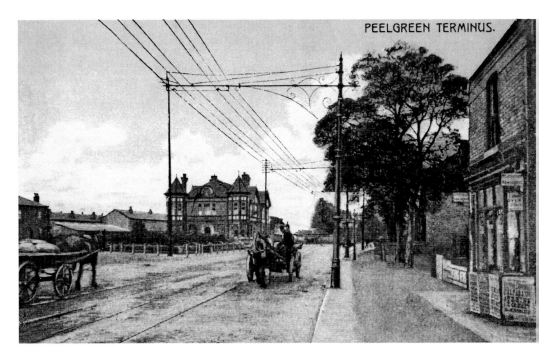

Peel Green Tram Terminus, from Liverpool Road, c. 1905
Peel Green is known for its cemetery (inset, crematorium), which was opened in 1879, covering 32 acres, with over 43,000 interments. The site was purchased in Autumn 1877 from the Bridgewater Trustees, for a yearly rental of £300. Originally located on the edge of Chat Moss, it is 2 miles west of Eccles. The first burial at Peel Green Cemetery was Amelia Mills, who died on 14 July 1879, aged seventy, was buried two days later and had lived at No. 518 Peel Green.

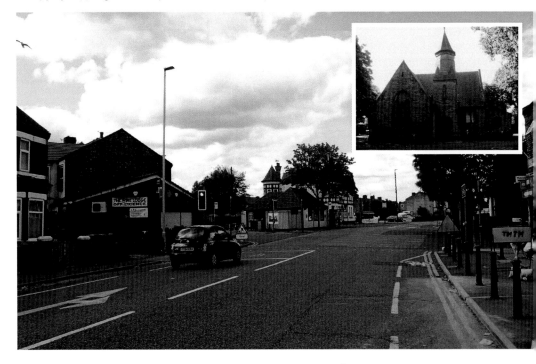

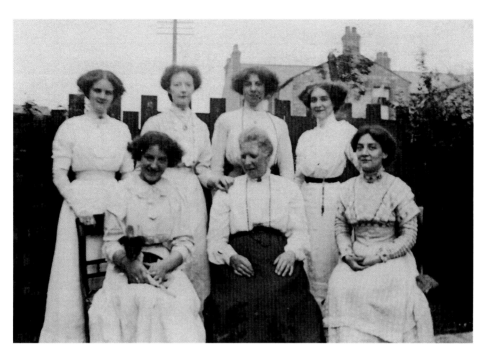

The Wilkinson Family, No. 111 Trafford Road (inset, centre), Eccles, 1911–12
There are two photographs, one of which has 'Laugh and grow fat', written on the back of it, while the other is addressed to Miss Wilkinson, 2 Beechwood Street, Great Lever, Bolton – the family had connections to this area of Lancashire. The rest of the text intriguingly reads, 'you will see I have got back to my castle again. Hope you did not get in trouble on Sunday,' and concludes, '... be pleased to see you both any time only let me know when.'

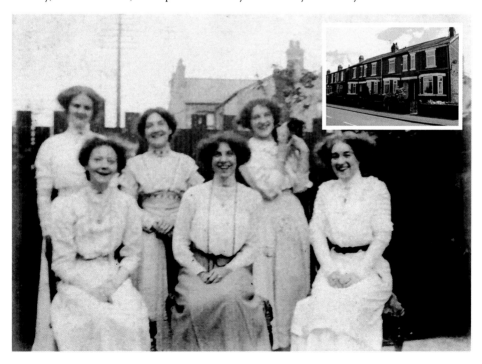

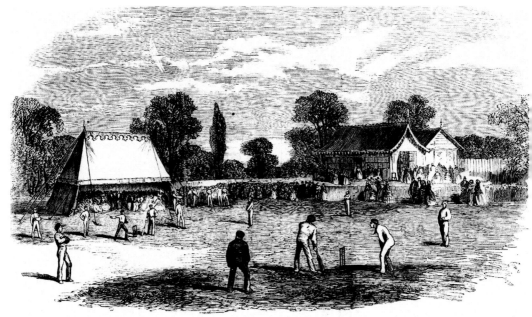

THE NEW CRICKET-GROUND, MANCHESTER.

The New Cricket Ground at Eccles, 13 June 1857

The 'Western Club' began playing at their new cricket ground in Eccles on Saturday 23 May 1857. In addition to the cricket pitch, both bowls and quoits were played. A pavilion of corrugated iron was erected for the use of members by Messrs. Edward T. Bellhouse & Co., of Manchester. It contained a dining room and some half-dozen smaller rooms, with around £1,000 being spent on preparing the ground and building the pavilion. Eccles Recreation Ground, on Oxford Street, now occupies the site.

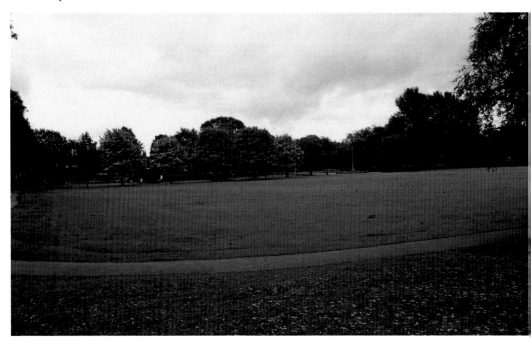

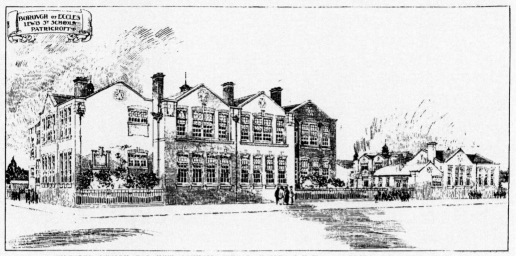

SELECTED DESIGN FOR NEW COUNCIL SCHOOL, ECCLES.—J. H. Woodhouse, F.R.I.B.A.,- Architect. (See page 500.)

Lewis Street Primary School, Patricroft, 27 April 1906

Opened in 1905, Lewis Street was the first Board Primary School in Salford. A former headmaster of the primary school was R. H. Lowe, once a pupil at Eccles Grammar School. Frederick Alexander Murdoch, formerly a teacher at Lewis Street, is a casualty of the Great War. He was a Private in the 20th Battalion Royal Fusiliers. Born on 26 July 1890, he died on 21 July 1916, aged twenty-five. Frederick is buried at Heilly Station Cemetery, Mericourt-L'abbe, France.

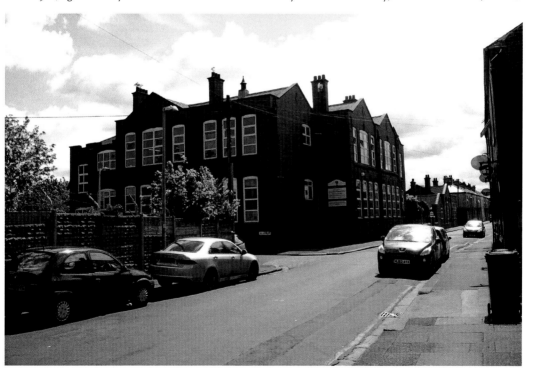

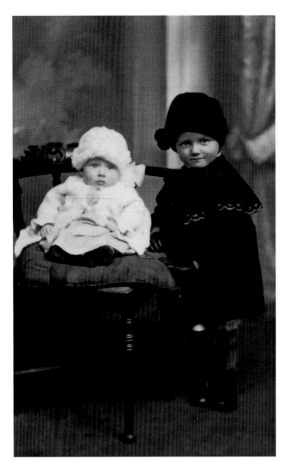

Charles Goddard Photography Studios, No. 118 Liverpool Road, Patricroft, c. 1900
This postcard photograph of two Victorian children is taken by the Patricroft photographer Charles Goddard, whose studios were located at No. 118 Liverpool Road. This is a fairly typical print of the time and illustrates very clearly the styles and fashions of Patricroft children in this era. They have probably been put in their 'Sunday best', especially for this particular portrait. The modern photograph and inset show the former Crown music hall, cinema and bingo hall, on Liverpool Road, looking towards Irlam.

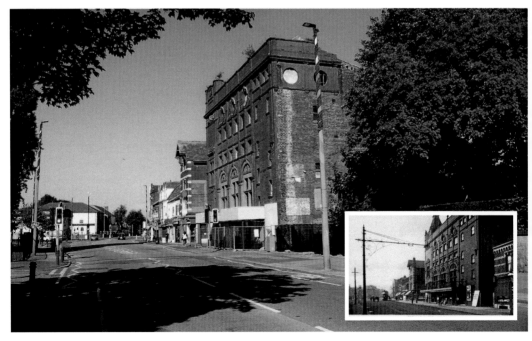

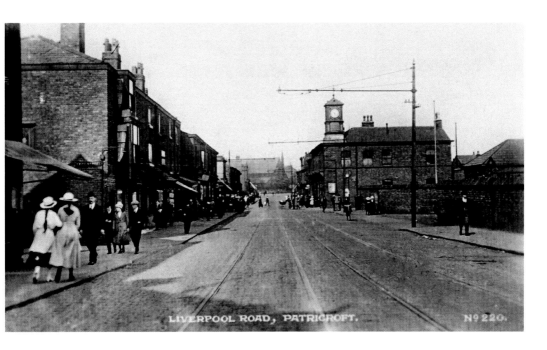

Liverpool Road, Junction with Legh Street, Looking Towards Christ Church (inset), Patricroft, 1932
Liverpool Road, Patricroft, begins at its junction with Church Street, Eccles, and ends beyond Barton Aerodrome (City Airport Manchester), heading towards Irlam. For much of its length, it consisted of shops, banks and other retail developments, including many public houses. Sir John Moores (1896–1993), the pools tycoon responsible for the development of the Littlewoods Co., was born above a public house on Liverpool Road, and A. V. Roe (1877–1958), the first Briton to construct and fly an aeroplane in 1908, was born at No. 262.

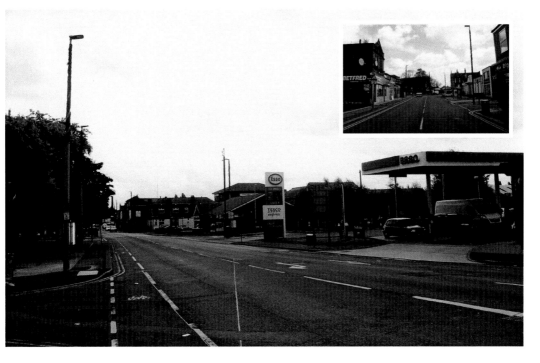

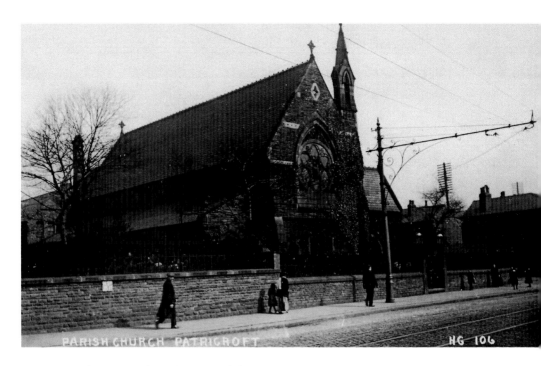

Christ Church, Liverpool Road, Patricroft, 1904
The parish was originally at the heart of the Industrial Revolution's expansion, which has now given way to light industry, alongside housing and a population of approximately 4,000. Christ Church was founded in 1868 and was intended to have a steeple, which was never constructed. It had seating for 750, until alterations in 1961. The organ was built in 1897 by James Jepson Binns of Leeds. The current church day and Sunday school buildings were built and opened in 1872.

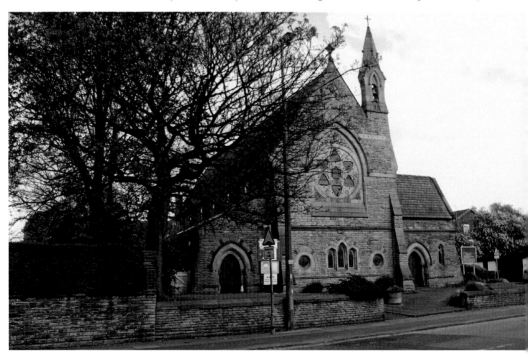

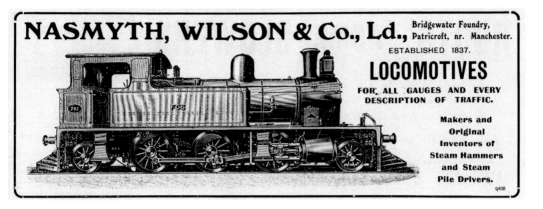

NASMYTH, WILSON & Co., Ld., Bridgewater Foundry, Patricroft, nr. Manchester.

ESTABLISHED 1837.

LOCOMOTIVES

FOR ALL GAUGES AND EVERY DESCRIPTION OF TRAFFIC.

Makers and Original Inventors of Steam Hammers and Steam Pile Drivers.

Nasmyth, Wilson & Co., Bridgewater Foundry Site, Junction of Green Lane and James Nasmyth Way, Patricroft

Adopted this name in 1867, after three previous titles and remained the company name until the firm went into liquidation, around 1939. They were one of the first factories to be established in Patricroft, at the Bridgewater Foundry, moving from Dale Street, Manchester, in 1836. The Foundry (inset) was located close to where the railway and canal crossed, with the company well known for building railway locomotives from 1838 and, from the mid-nineteenth century, steam hammers, which were developed by James Nasmyth.

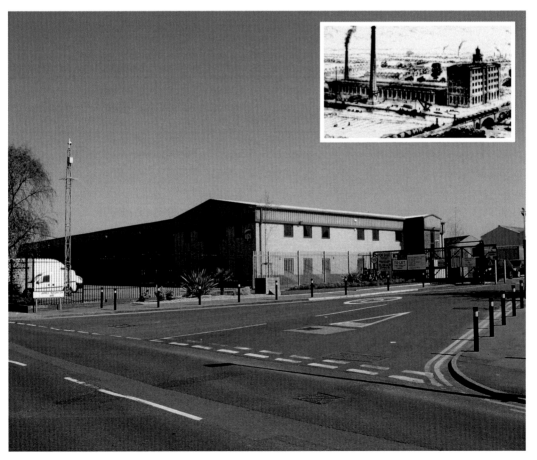

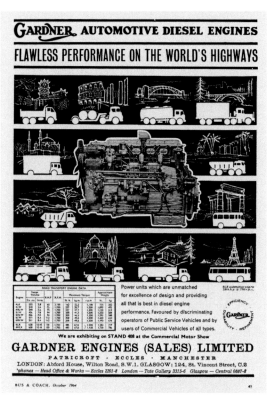

Gardner Engines Ltd, Barton Hall Engine Works, Hardy Street, Patricroft, 1964

Around 1868, Lawrence Gardner set up as a sewing machine maker in Hulme. He died in 1890, but his sons continued the business as L. Gardner & Sons Ltd. From 1895, the company built gas engines and in 1899 moved into Barton Hall Engine Works, Patricroft. Diesel engines were produced here from c. 1903, and by 1910, Gardners employed 1,000 workers, occupying 8 acres of land. In the summer of 1986, Perkins Engines purchased the company, which ceased production in the early 1990s.

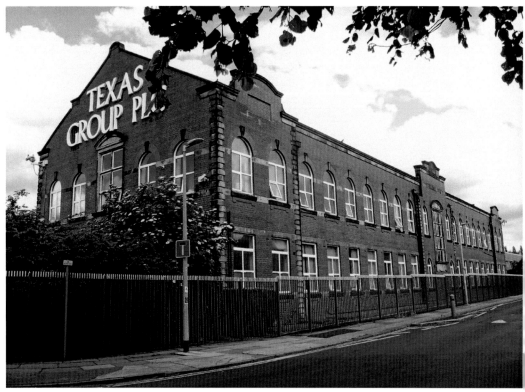

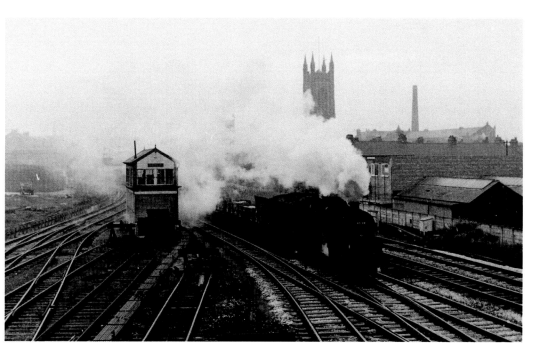

Freight Passing Through Patricroft Yard and St Andrew's Church, Eccles, 22 October 1966
Situated behind Patricroft railway station, on the Manchester platform side of the line, was a large power depot – Patricroft Yard – with steam sheds, which ceased all activities in 1968. Patricroft is located on the original Liverpool–Manchester passenger railway, a major feat of engineering across Chat Moss, constructed by George Stephenson and opened in 1830. All the station buildings were demolished in the 1980s, but it remains the only railway station in the area with direct access to the Bridgewater Canal.

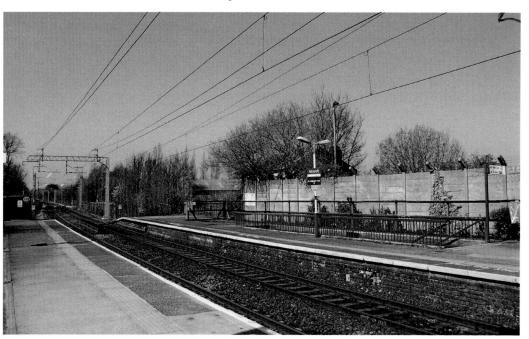

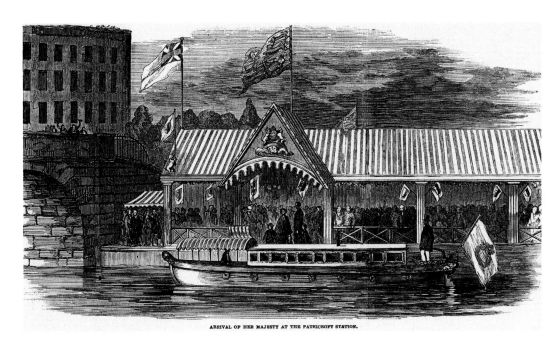

ARRIVAL OF HER MAJESTY AT THE PATRICROFT STATION.

Queen Victoria Boarding the Royal Barge at Patricroft Railway Station, Green Lane, 1851
The Queen's Arms (inset) was opened in 1828 and claims to be the world's first railway public house. Initially, it had direct access to the station but is now fenced off from it. It is said that Queen Victoria used the facilities here, after her arrival by train from Liverpool, in 1851. She then boarded the royal barge to Worsley, in order to be a guest of the Earl of Ellesmere. Originally the Patricroft Tavern, it became the Queen's Arms after Victoria's visit.

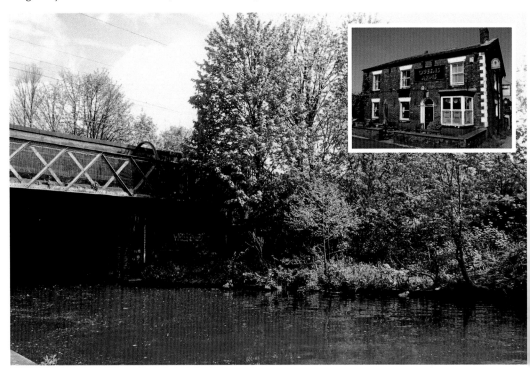

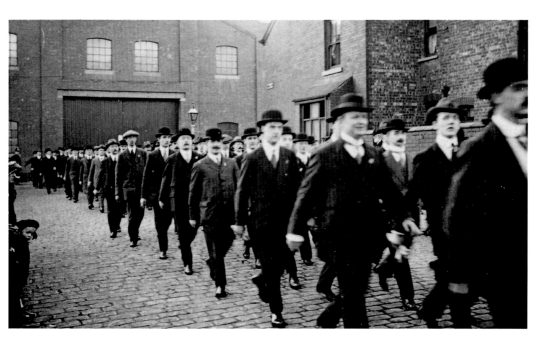

Church Parade, Pym Street, Patricroft, Sunday 2 August 1914

The handwritten notes on the back of this photograph state that it was 'Taken on parade to church. Not bad is it as we were marching. Give this one to the youngsters'. The gentlemen in this photograph are dressed in their 'Sunday best' and are marching down Pym Street, towards Vane Street, on their way to Christ Church, Patricroft, on Liverpool Road. The date is significant, as only two days later, on 4 August 1914, Britain declared war on Germany.

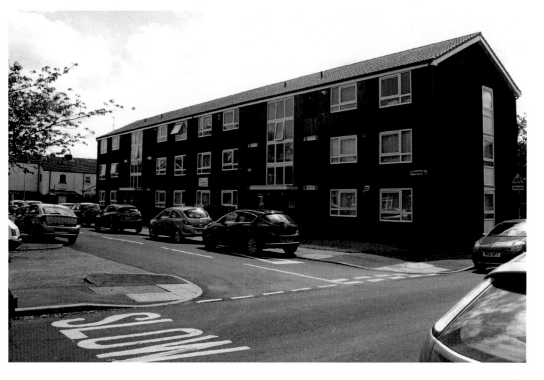

67

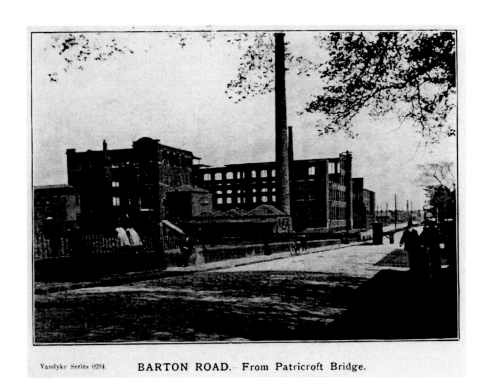

Vandyke Series 0284. **BARTON ROAD. From Patricroft Bridge.**

Barton Road from Patricroft Bridge, 1919, and the Packet House (inset), 2015
Patricroft Bridge contains the earliest section of the Bridgewater Canal, leading to the development of the cotton industry along its banks. The ability to transport coal for power led to a cluster of cotton mills, particularly between Monton and the Barton Aqueduct. Opposite Barton Road (pictured), on the east bank, there were more cotton mills served by their own wharfs. The one in the photograph is in the process of being demolished in 1919. The present road bridge dates from 1961.

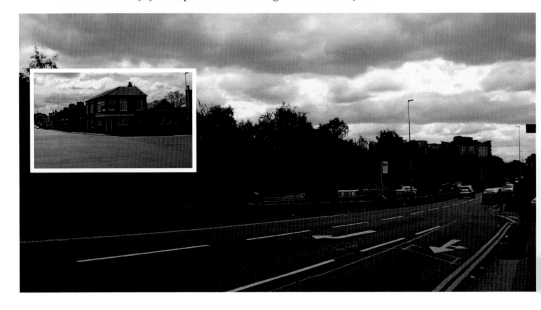

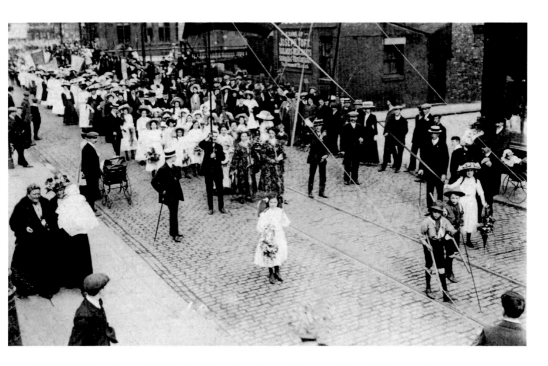

Whit Walks at Joseph Toft, Builders Merchants, Liverpool Road, Patricroft, c. 1905
The 1881 Census lists Joseph Toft as aged twenty-four and married to Margaret Toft. His occupation is given as a slate and timber merchant, and he is living at No. 434 Liverpool Road, Barton-upon-Irwell. Forty years later, the family is still in the area, with a wedding registered at St Catherine's church, Barton-upon-Irwell, on 19 September 1922, between John Rossall Evans and Florrie Toft, aged twenty-seven and of Elton Place. Her father is Joseph Toft, a builder's merchant.

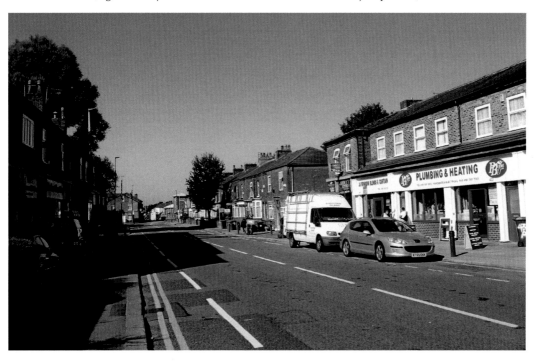

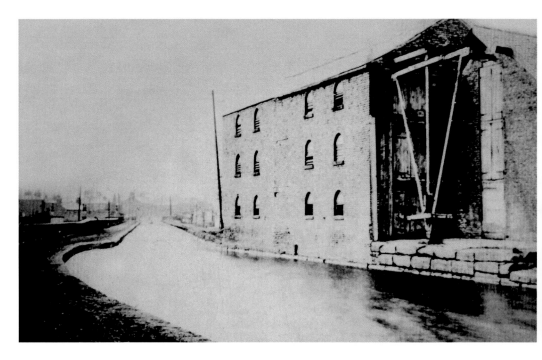

Bridgewater Canal and a Warehouse, c. 1890, and Bridgewater Mill, 2015, at Patricroft
Francis Egerton, the Third Duke of Bridgewater, built the canal in order to transport coal from his mines at Worsley to the industrial areas of Manchester. It is often referred to as the forerunner of canal networks. The Duke promised to reduce the delivered price of coal in Manchester to no more than 4*d* per hundred weight, thus guaranteeing support from local merchants. As the canal extended, warehouses like this one at Patricroft were constructed in order to store coal and other goods.

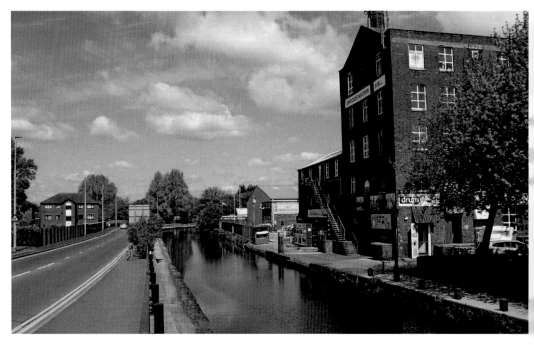

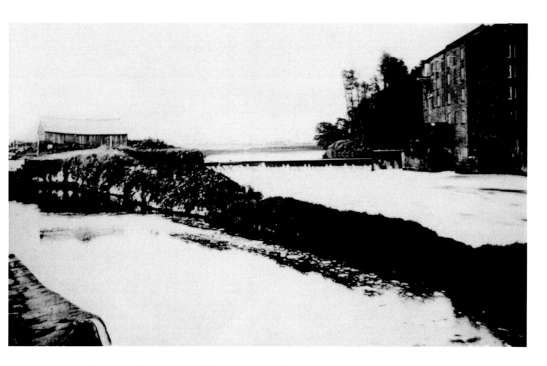

Barton Before the Manchester Ship Canal, c. 1880
The Rivers Mersey and Irwell were made fully navigable from Warrington to Manchester by the Mersey and Irwell Navigation Co. Barges with a maximum length of approximately 66 feet and a maximum width of approximately 16 feet were using this section of the river by 1734. Known as 'Mersey Flats', these barges were specially constructed to negotiate the treacherous riverbeds and fast-flowing currents of the Mersey and Irwell. Navigation was improved by short canal sections and the construction of weirs.

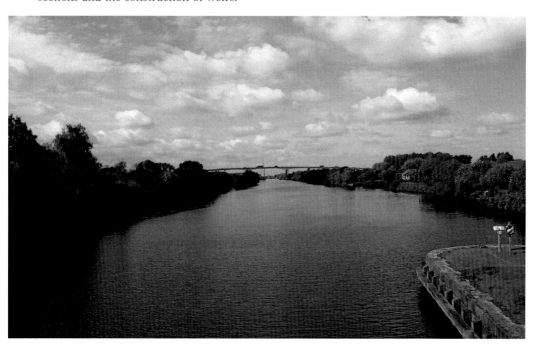

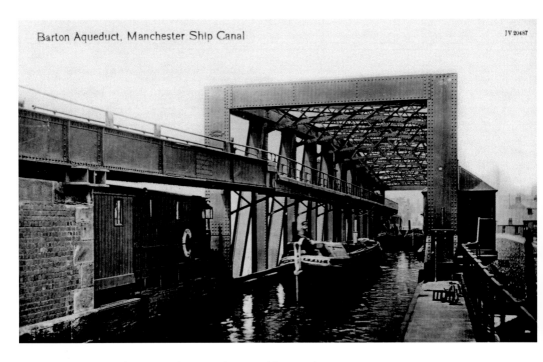

Barton Swing Aqueduct over the Manchester Ship Canal, 1914

It is 235 feet long and weighs 1,450 tons. The bridge swings on a central axis to allow the passage of ships. The aqueduct takes the form of a boxed lattice girder, containing an upper section, the channel remaining full of water when turning. James Brindley (1716–72) designed the Bridgewater Canal, his stone aqueduct being built *c.* 1761 and replaced in *c.* 1891. There are remains of this aqueduct preserved on the Eccles side of the Manchester Ship Canal (inset) and marked by a plaque.

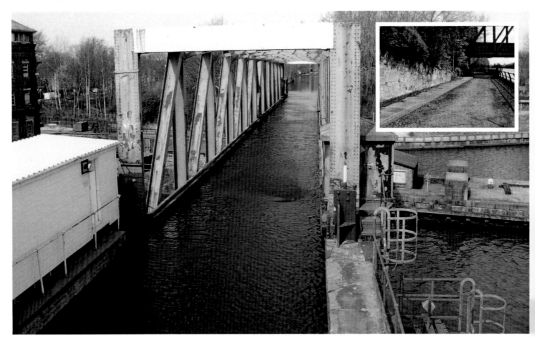

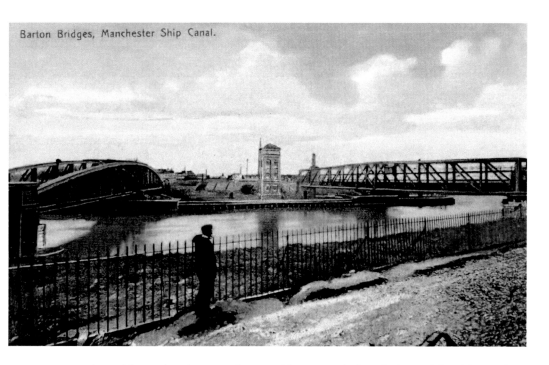

Barton Bridges, Manchester Ship Canal.

Barton Swing Bridge and Swing Aqueduct, Looking Towards foundations of the old Aqueduct, *c.* **1909**

Barton swing bridge was constructed *c.* 1893, with the bridge, aqueduct (inset, original aqueduct) and control tower Grade II listed in 1987. The engineer was Sir Edward Leader Williams (1828–1910), Andrew Handyside & Co., providing the materials. It weighs 800 tons and is 195 feet long and 25 feet wide. It has a sixty-four roller hydraulic system, enabling it to revolve on a central axis, allowing the passage of ships. These often expanded in heat, causing the structure to lock and the travelling public to be 'bridged'.

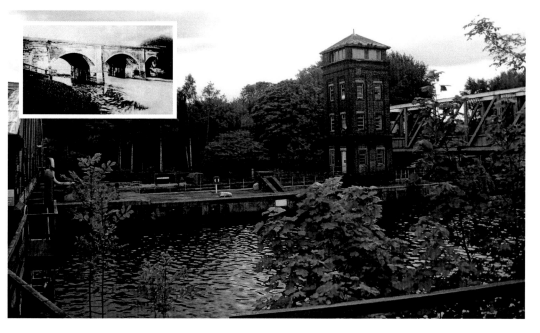

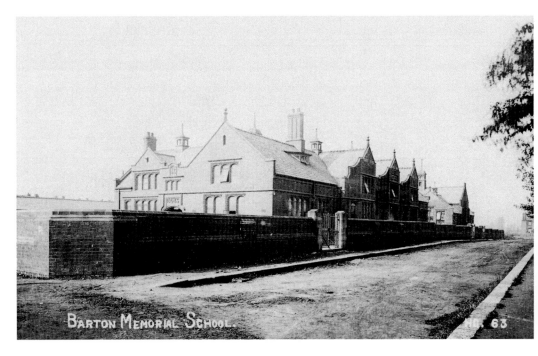

Barton (Godfrey Ermen) Memorial School, School Road, Eccles, 1905

Godfrey Ermen was a Victorian mill owner who left a bequest in his will to fund the construction of the Barton Memorial School, later Godfrey Ermen Memorial School, in 1903. Ermen owned mills at Weaste and Eccles, trading under the name of Ermen & Engels – later Ermen & Roby. The firm was bought out by the English Sewing Cotton Co., in 1897. At that time the company had mills in Patricroft and Pendlebury, employing around 1,200 people. The Patricroft mill closed c. 1945.

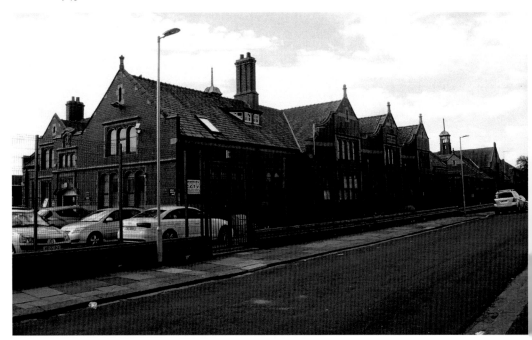

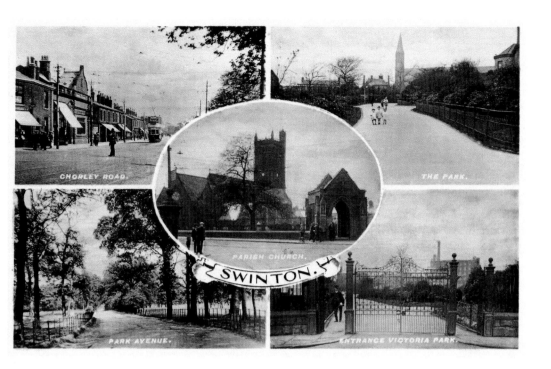

Chorley Road, Victoria Park, St Peter's Church, Park Avenue, and Entrance to Victoria Park, c. 1910 and 2015

The name Swinton derives from the Old English 'swin' meaning 'pigs' and 'tun' meaning 'an enclosure', 'farmstead' or 'manor'. Land belonged to Whalley Abbey, the Knights Hospitallers and, later, Thurston Tyldesley of Wardley Hall. The growth of factories and urbanisation led Swinton to become an important mining and mill town. The photograph at the bottom right of the postcard, showing the entrance to Victoria Park, also shows the Albion Cotton Mill, at Pendlebury and its distinctive chimney silhouetted against the Salford skyline.

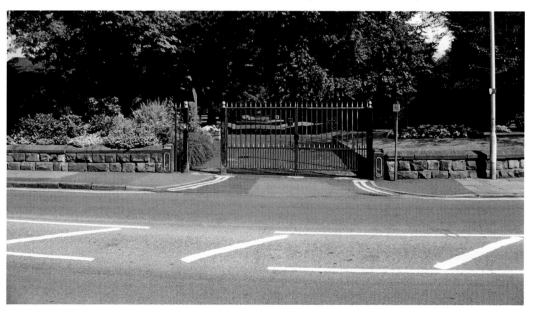

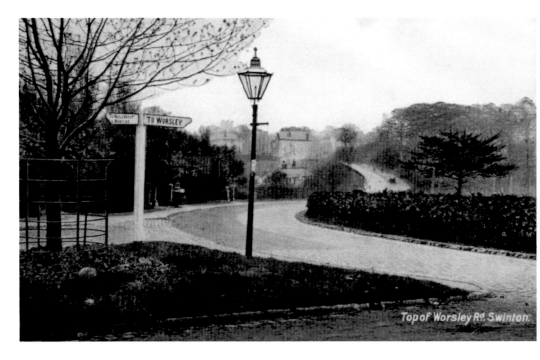

Top of Worsley Road, Swinton, Looking Towards Swinton, c. 1905

This view of the top of Worsley Road, Swinton looks towards the town of Swinton and Swinton Park, with Hazlehurst and Moorside, the destinations of the junction to the left of the photograph, along Moorside Road. This area has changed from one of a semi-rural outlook to one of mainly residential properties, built from c. 1930. Worsley Road is now a busy main road heading towards its junction with the M60 motorway at Worsley, close to the boundary with Swinton.

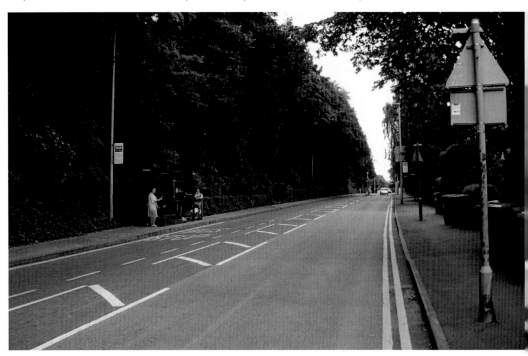

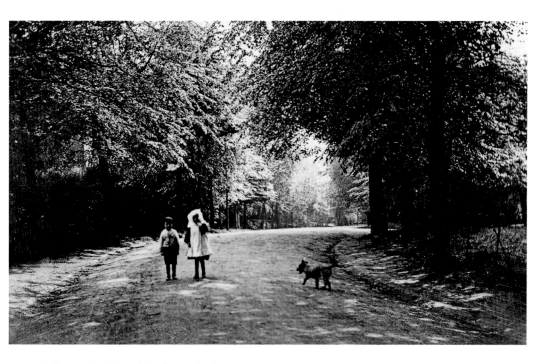

Radcliffe Park Road, Swinton Park, 1905

In 1905, Radcliffe Park Road (now Salford) was a country lane, whose path took it through the open countryside of Swinton Park. Today the road is along the boundary of what remains of Swinton Park and is one of a number of residential roads that now cover this section of the former recreational space. In 1905, it was a very rural and tranquil scene, the route being used to provide direct access to the park, where it then petered out into a 'dead end'.

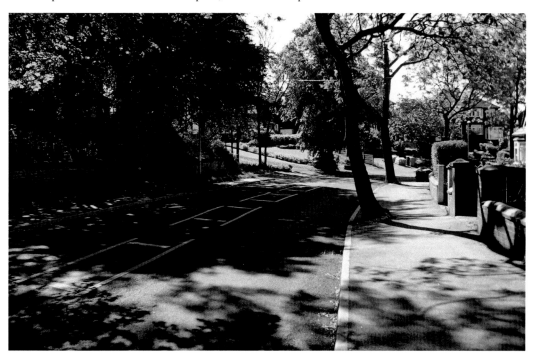

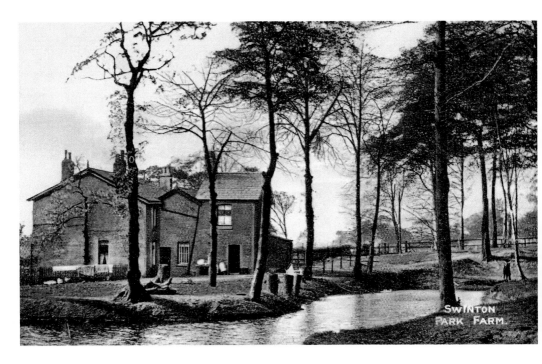

Former Swinton Park Farm c. 1900 and Golf Course Clubhouse from Cliftonville Drive, 2015, Road, c. 1900

Swinton Park was originally a large country park, containing Swinton House, well-kept gardens and an associated farm – Swinton Park Farm (inset) – to the south of Manchester Road. The park forms the western end of an arc of estates in this area, extending north-east to Pendlebury House. Apart from the farm, there were a number of associated dwellings to the south and east of Swinton House. By the late nineteenth century, the park was being earmarked for industrial and housing development.

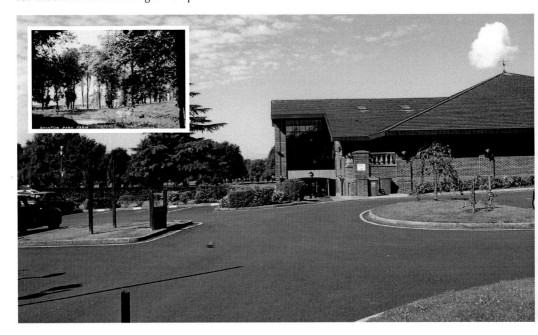

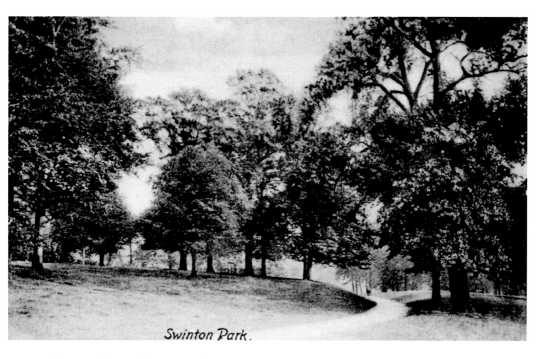

Swinton Park.

Swinton Park, Manchester Road, Swinton, 1905

Swinton Park, adjacent to the East Lancashire Road, is now the home of Swinton Park Golf Club, a private parkland course laid out in 1926 by the famous golfer and course designer, James Braid. It was designed with tree-lined fairways and wide, open greens, to be used by golfers of all abilities. It is regarded by many to be a top-class course and with a capacity of 6,726 yards and is reputed to be one of the longest and best in the area.

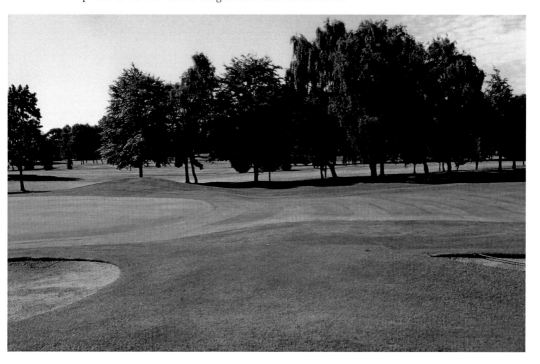

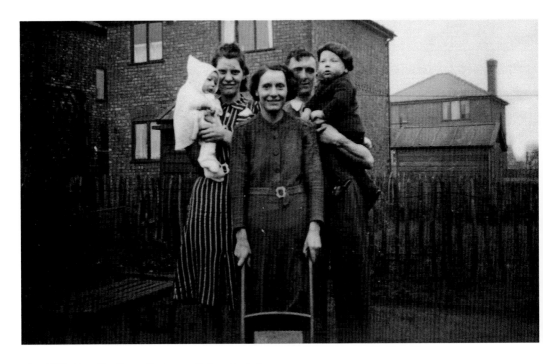

The Cliffe Family, No. 9 Parkgate Drive, Swinton, 1939
The interwar years saw a tremendous growth in the construction of residential properties throughout the United Kingdom. In the case of Swinton, large areas to the south of the district were earmarked for residential development, particularly around Swinton Park. The above photograph shows the Cliffe family (and inset), in the back garden of No. 9 Parkgate Drive, which still looks relatively newly constructed, as the gardens have yet to mature. The family relocated to Davyhulme shortly after this photograph was taken.

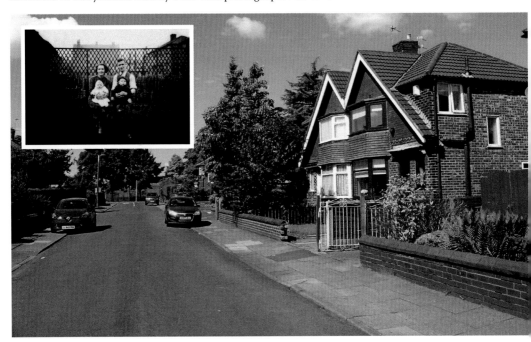

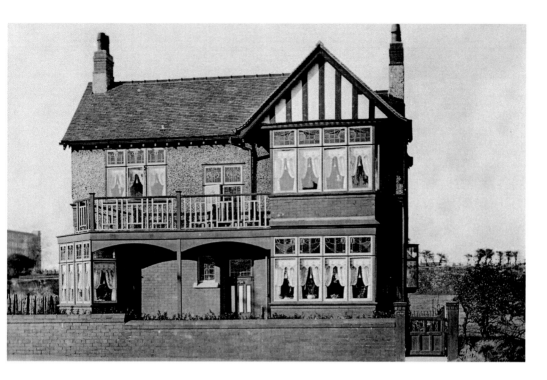

Property on Manchester Road, Swinton, c. 1930
The interwar expansion of Swinton's housing stock and the construction of new roads in the area, as shown in the photograph of Manchester Road above, was stimulated by the development of brick works in the area, providing the necessary raw materials. Manchester Road becomes Chorley Road at its junction with Worsley Road and runs parallel to the A580, East Lancashire Road to Liverpool (inset) – the United Kingdom's first purpose-built inter-city highway. It was officially opened by King George V, 18 July 1934.

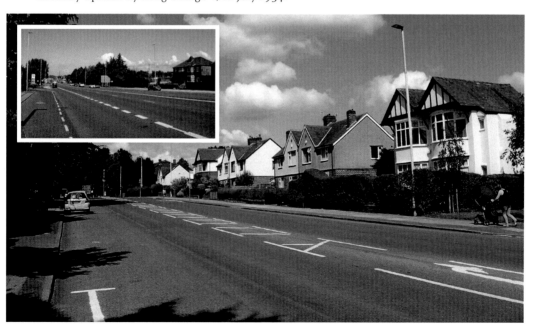

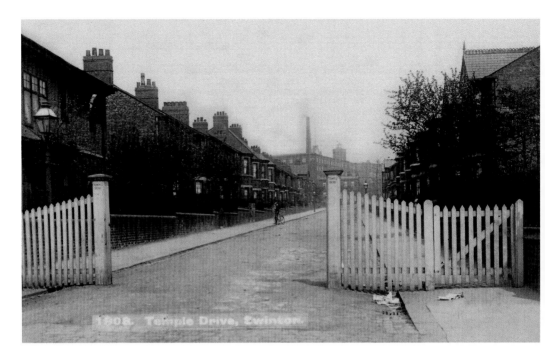

Temple Drive, Swinton, c. 1910

Clifton Hall Tunnel, known locally as 'Black Harry', was a railway tunnel that passed beneath Temple Drive. On Tuesday 28 April 1953, it partially collapsed around an old brick-lined construction shaft, killing five residents of Temple Drive, at Nos 22 and 24, which were completely destroyed (inset). The end wall of No. 26 also collapsed, although the occupants survived. The tunnel was later filled with colliery waste, but there continues to be ground movement and subsidence in the area to this day.

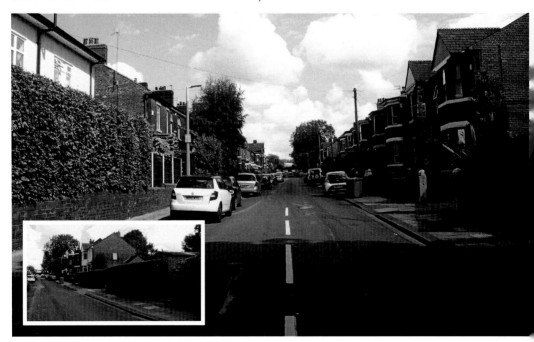

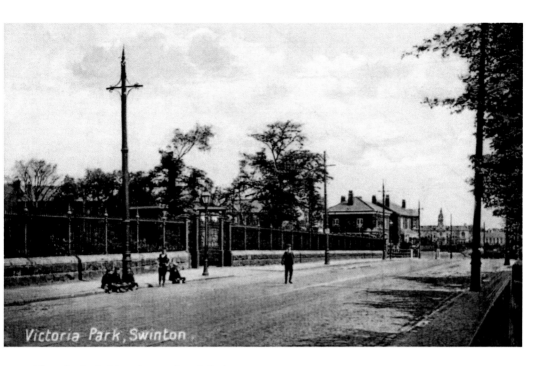

Victoria Park, Manchester Road, Swinton, *c.* 1905
Victoria Park opened in 1897, on land purchased by the urban districts of Swinton and Pendlebury. The park is made up of the grounds of Swinton Old Hall, the hall itself being demolished in 1993. It has among its facilities tennis courts and two bowling greens and is home to a Grade II listed Victorian bandstand. On 29 September 1934, Swinton and Pendlebury received its Charter of Incorporation as a municipal borough from Edward Stanley, 18th Earl of Derby, at a ceremony in Victoria Park.

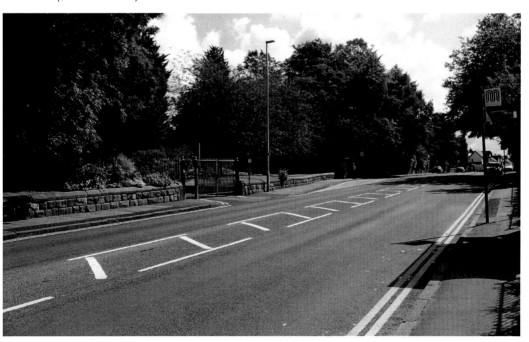

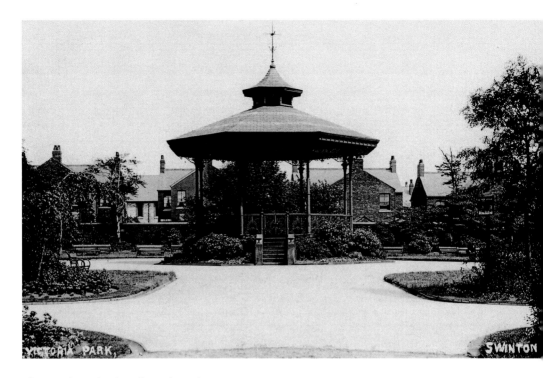

The Bandstand, Victoria Park, Swinton, *c.* 1900

The now restored bandstand was constructed to commemorate the sixtieth anniversary of the reign of Queen Victoria and is a Grade II listed structure. The bandstand has recently been the location of several live music events, which are suited to the location. It is situated in one of the most popular parks in Salford. Victoria Park is the recipient of a Green Flag Award and has well maintained floral displays throughout the year, as well as a range of diverse activities.

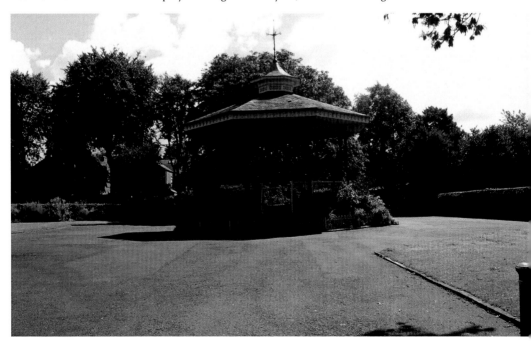

C. Musker Bros Ltd, Bingham Street, Swinton, 1942
Musker Bros Ltd was a family run firm and an established building contractor through several generations, including Thomas, James and Wright Musker. Many are buried at Swinton Cemetery (inset). The above advert states that the company were 'contractors to the Cheshire County Council' and probably benefitted from the interwar demand for housing contractors. The housing stock in Swinton also increased in the same period, with the town becoming a popular suburban location, close to the cities of Salford and Manchester.

INFORMATION ABOUT

FACTORY SITES

BESIDE THE

MANCHESTER SHIP CANAL

AND THE

BRIDGEWATER CANAL

may be obtained from the Manchester Ship Canal Company's Land Agents

DUNLOP & COMPANY

82 BRAZENNOSE STREET

MANCHESTER   ENGLAND

Telephone : SWINTON 1809 and 1520

C. MUSKER BROS. LTD.

Bingham Street, SWINTON, Manchester

GENERAL BUILDING CONTRACTORS

AND MANUFACTURERS OF THE

Armoured Tubular
Concrete Floors and Roofs

FLOOR SECTIONS delivered to site ready for fixing, no shuttering required, fixed one day, ready for use the next, showing no delay to job progress, ceilings ready to receive plaster ceiling direct.

Contractors to the Cheshire County Council

[244]

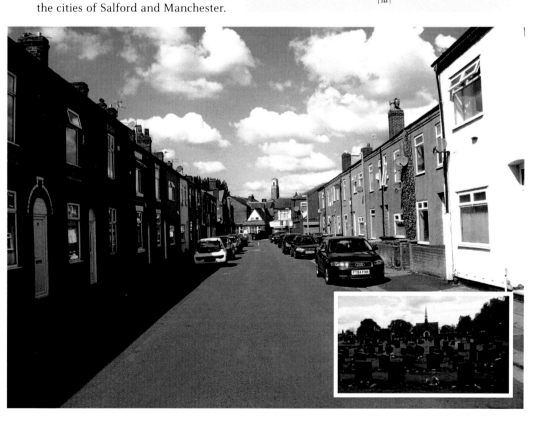

85

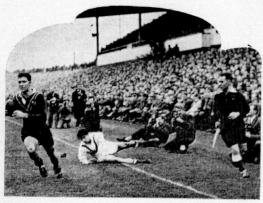

SWINTON

VERSUS

WAKEFIELD T.

TEST MATCH AT SWINTON OCTOBER 17th
Photograph by kind permission of Lancashire Evening Post

OFFICIAL PROGRAMME Price 3d.

Swinton *v.* Wakefield Trinity, 5 December 1959 (Cover Features Great Britain (24) *v.* Australia (25), 17 October 1959) and Station Road, 2015
Swinton RLFC joined the new Northern Union on 2 June 1896. The club enjoyed a certain amount of success, especially in the 1920s and 1930s (inset 1934/35). They won the Lancashire Cup in 1925; won the Challenge Cup in 1926; secured their first Championship in 1927; and in 1928 became the last team to win all four cups (Championship trophy , Challenge Cup, Lancashire League and Lancashire Cup), in the same season. They also won a fifth trophy, the Salford Royal Hospital Cup.

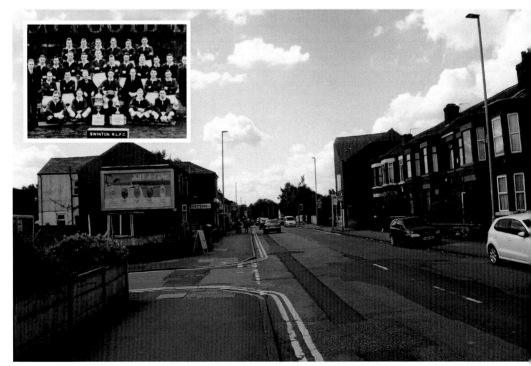

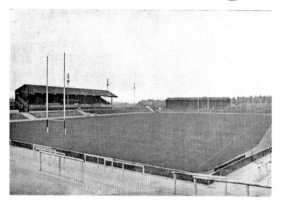

SWINTON
FOOTBALL CLUB
CO. LTD.

Ground: STATION ROAD . SWINTON

LANCASHIRE COUNTY CHALLENGE CUP FIRST ROUND

SWINTON v. WORKINGTON T.

OFFICIAL PROGRAMME 6D

Swinton 11 Workington 14, Station Road, Saturday 6 September 1968, and Station Road, 2015

Swinton Lions now play at Sedgeley Park RUFC, Whitefield. Championship winners six times and Challenge Cup winners three times, they were formed 21 October 1866 and joined the Rugby Football Union as Swinton and Pendlebury FC, based at Station Road. In 1873, they moved to 'Stoneacre', using the White Lion public house as changing rooms and adopting the 'Lions' as their nickname. In 1886, they moved to Chorley Road, moving back to No. 66 Station Road, 1929, which was sold for property development, 1992.

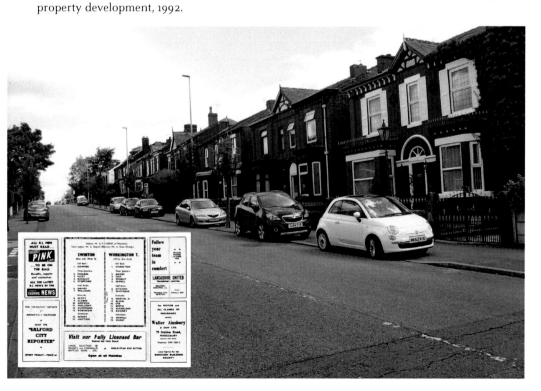

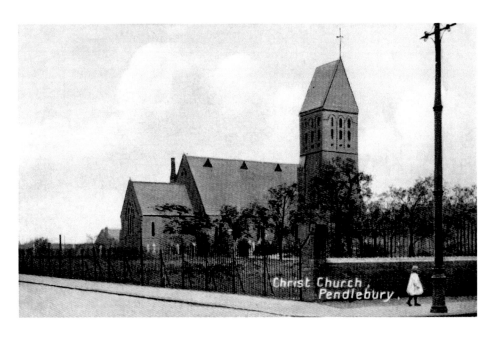

Christ Church, Pendlebury, *c.* 1910

Christ Church was completed and consecrated on 24 December 1859, costing £3,000, raised by subscription. The architect was W. R. Corson of St James Square, Manchester. Built on a corner plot, at the junction of Bolton Road and Pendlebury Road, the church seated 587. In 1861, the church tower was added, costing £1,095, and in 1880, the vicarage was built, costing £2,028. In 1863, a day school opened, and in January 1868, the first peel of eight bells was rung at Christ Church.

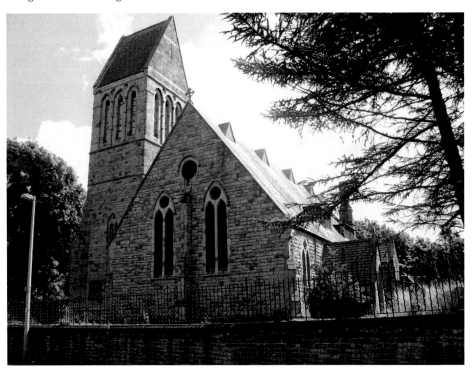

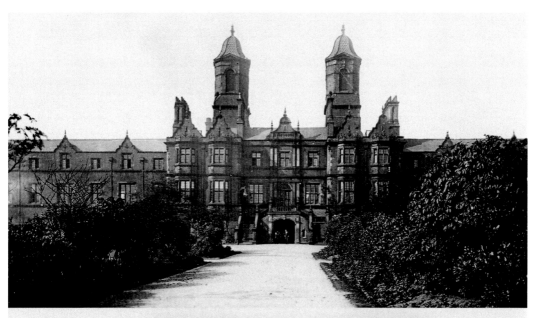

SWINTON INDUSTRIAL SCHOOLS, MANCHESTER.

Swinton Industrial Schools, Chorley Road, Swinton, c. 1905

Manchester was one of the first unions to set up large separate institutions for pauper children. The school was erected in 1843–45 and was designed by Richard Tattersall. It was a long, three storey, T-shaped building, with two tall towers and Dutch gables. There were separate Anglican and Roman Catholic chapels, erected at either end of the site. Charles Dickens visited and wrote about the school in 1850. The building was demolished and replaced by the town hall (Salford Civic Centre), in 1937.

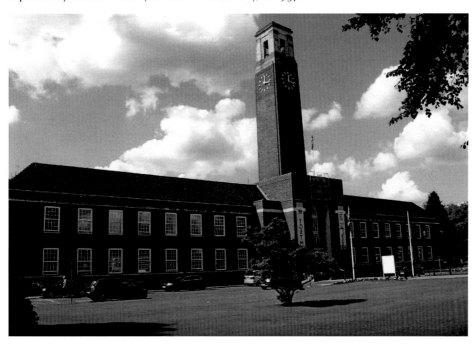

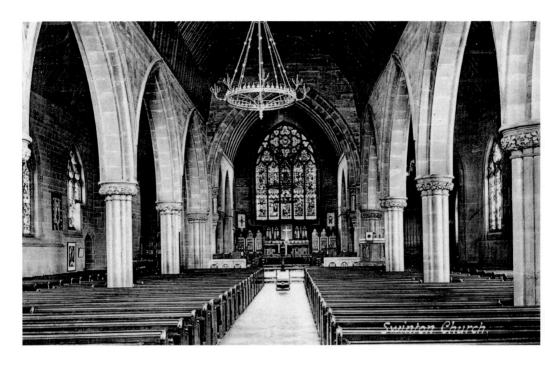

Interior of St Peter's Parish Church, Junction of Chorley Road and Partington Lane, Swinton, c. 1900

Swinton was historically a part of the parish of Eccles, with a chapel built in Swinton, 1791. It became Swinton parish, 1865, with the Revd Henry Robinson appointed vicar. A new church was completed, 1870, to replace the chapel, and in 1887, a decision was taken to build a new school on Vicarage Road. Noah Robinson (1826–1907), philanthropist and founding father of modern Swinton, is commemorated in a memorial window of October 1909 and on the lychgate (inset), to St Peter's.

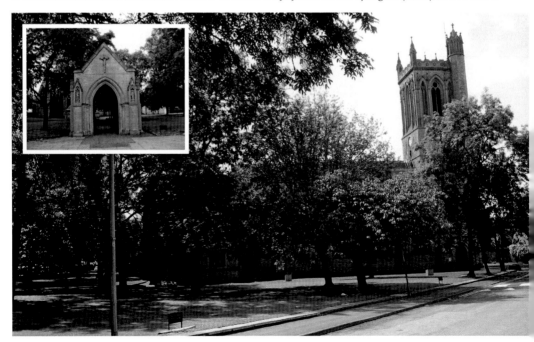

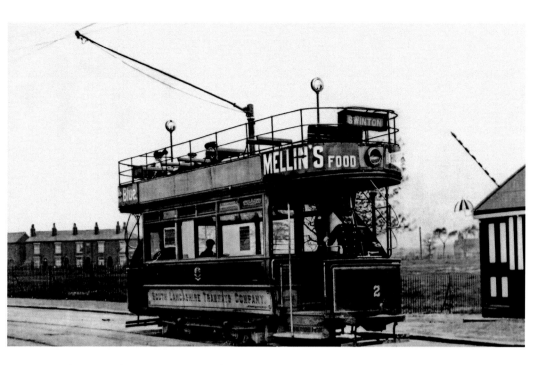

Tram from Mosley Common to Swinton, *c.* 1910, and Chorley Road Junction with Partington Lane (left), 2015

The headquarters of the South Lancashire Tramways and the Lancashire United Tramways Ltd was at Atherton, near Leigh, in South Lancashire. The tram above has been photographed at Mosley Common, which was a suburb of Tyldesley, with a final destination of Swinton, via Worsley, at the junction of Partington Lane and Chorley Road (inset). After 1906, this service was extended to neighbouring Walkden. Services were due to be stopped in 1938, but the war meant that it was November 1944 before they ceased.

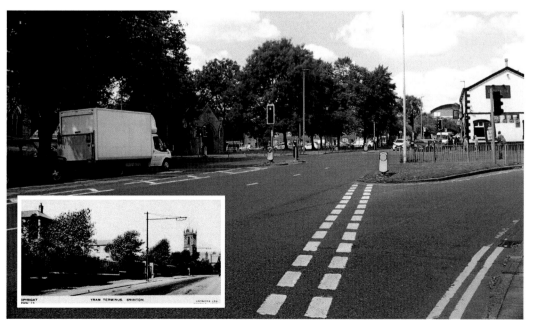

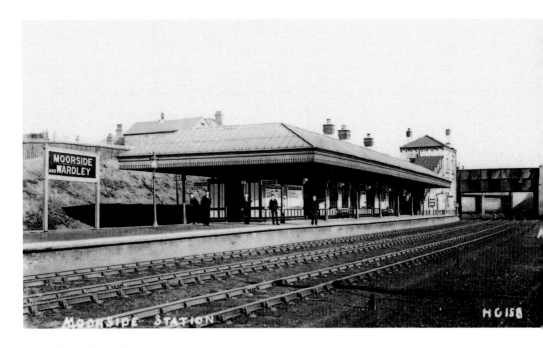

Moorside Railway Station, Moorside Road, Swinton, c. 1910

The station is located in the Moorside and Wardley areas of Swinton. Until 6 May 1974, the railway station was named Moorside and Wardley, becoming Moorside on that date. It is the least used station on the Atherton line, which runs between Wigan and Manchester Victoria. There are regular Northern Rail services to Salford, Walkden, Atherton and Hindley. Two minutes to the east of Moorside station is Swinton station (inset), which retains its original canopy and the cast iron pillars supporting it.

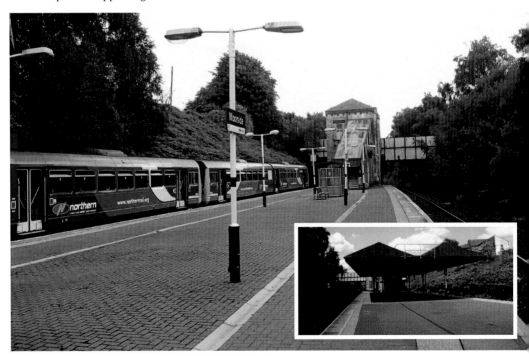

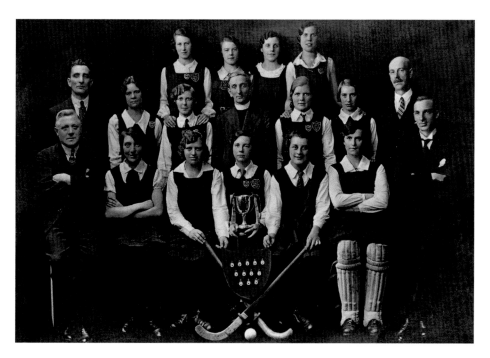

Swinton All Saints Hockey Club, Charles Street, Wardley (FLHL Finalists 1927)
The church of All Saints in the parish of Swinton and Pendlebury was built by Bernard Oliver Francis Heywood, in 1914. The parish church is St Peter's, Swinton, with another district church, St Augustine's (inset), at Bolton Road, Pendlebury, known as the 'Miner's Cathedral', with a memorial to sixty-four victims of the Clifton Hall Colliery explosion, of 18 June 1885. The photograph of 1927 has a handwritten note on the back, which reads, 'Yours sincerely, A. Moore (Captain), Swinton All Saints Hockey Club.'

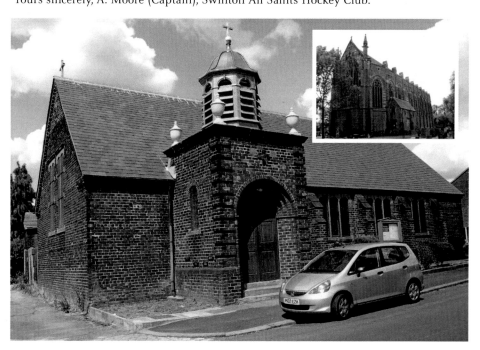

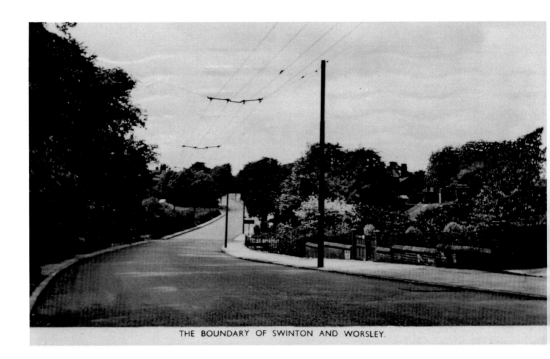

THE BOUNDARY OF SWINTON AND WORSLEY.

Swinton and Worsley Boundary, Worsley Road, Looking Towards Worsley, at Ringlow Park Road, 1951

In the nineteenth century, Swinton was part of Worsley township, in the parish of Eccles and Hundred of Salford, becoming an independent authority in the 1860s. The left of the photograph is now a garden centre, with Ringlow Park Road to the right. Also shown is the Swinton and Worsley boundary from the junction of Moorside Road and Chorley Road, at the Red Lion, looking towards Worsley (inset). Sindsley Brook marks the boundary between the old towns of Swinton and Worsley.

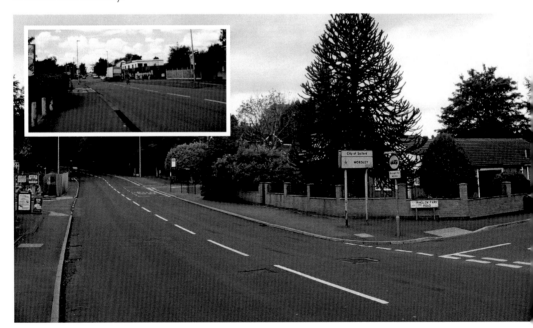

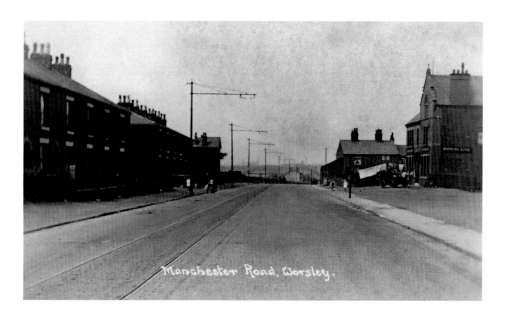

The Morning Star, Manchester Road, Worsley, c. 1930, and the Red Lion, Chorley Road, Swinton, 2015

The Wardley area of Swinton had three public houses, the Morning Star, the Red Lion and the Brook Tavern, on the Worsley side of Sindsley Brook and now a retail outlet. The Morning Star is situated in Worsley, but close to the boundary between Swinton and Worsley, as is its neighbour, the Red Lion (inset), situated in Swinton. The photograph above shows Manchester Road with tram lines, looking towards Wardley Old Hall and Worsley, where the M60 and M61 motorways now cross.

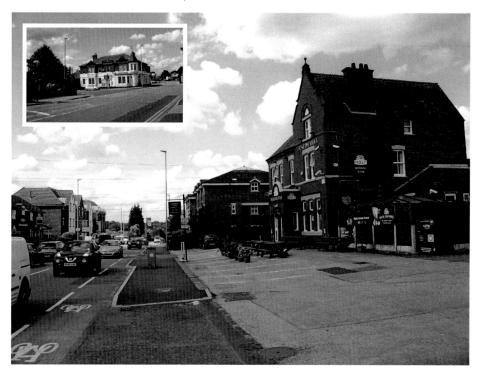

About the Author

Steven is the author of *Sale Through Time, Flixton, Urmston and Davyhulme Through Time, Stretford and Old Trafford Through Time* and *Victorian Manchester Through Time*. He has an academic background in modern history and is a retired charge nurse and college lecturer. He is married to Sarah. They have six children and live in the Flixton area of Manchester.

Bibliography

Hayes, C., *Francis Frith's Around Manchester* (Salisbury: Frith Book Co. Ltd, 2000).

Old Ordnance Survey Maps. Eccles, 1905 (Consett: Alan Godfrey Maps, 2003).

Old Ordnance Survey Maps. Patricroft & Monton, 1905 (Consett: Alan Godfrey Maps, 2006).

Old Ordnance Survey Maps. Swinton Park & Irlam o' th' Heights, 1907 (Newcastle upon Tyne: Alan Godfrey Maps, 1997).

Salford City Council (www.salford.gov.uk).

Swindells T., *Chapters in the History of Eccles* (Pendleton: Wilkinson, 1914).